# THE CHURCH ON THE WAY

# THE CHURCH ON THE WAY

## JACK W. HAYFORD

Learning to live in the promise
of biblical congregational life

√ chosen books

FLEMING H. REVELL COMPANY
OLD TAPPAN, NEW JERSEY

All Scripture quotations, unless otherwise designated, are the writer's adaptation of the King James Version (1611), which he has adjusted to read with fidelity to the text of that translation but with a more contemporary readability. Where the indication (Paraphrase) occurs, it is the author's own, based on his study of the Nestle Greek text.

The paragraph on p. 186 is from *A Severe Mercy*, by Sheldon Vanauken, © 1977 by Harper & Row, Publishers, Inc., and used with permission.

**Library of Congress Cataloging in Publication Data**
Hayford, Jack, W.
    The Church on the Way.
      1. Church on the Way (Van Nuys, CA)—History.
2. Church renewal—International Church of the
Foursquare Gospel—Case Studies.    3. Hayford, Jack W.
I. Title
BX7990.I67V3634    1982      289.9      82-19779
ISBN 0-8007-9072-3

A Chosen Book
**Copyright © 1983 by Jack Hayford**
Chosen Books are Published by
Fleming H. Revell Company
Old Tappan, New Jersey
Printed in the United States of America

# Acknowledgments

"In all thy ways acknowledge Him. . ." (Proverbs 3:6).

This story of God's grace in recent years at "The Church on the Way" is clearly a report of *His* doings with us, and I believe we have made that clear—the glory belongs to Jesus! But God's way of doing things always involves people as well, and the following are a few of those He has singularly used to bring all this about.

My praise to Him for and the deepest thanks of my heart to:

Anna, whose total commitment to our ministry together and whose completing love and untiring patience make her a biblical wife, "worth more than precious gems" (Proverbs 31:10 LB).

Jack and Dolores Hayford, whom I still unashamedly call "Daddy" and "Mama." He's with the Lord and she's with us at the church. They are the ones who first taught me to walk "on the way" with a steadfastness that would eventually influence others.

All the congregation of "The Church On the Way," for being willing to move as one people, committed to growing in Christ and His Word instead of only growing in numbers.

All the church's counsel, elders, deacons, teachers and workers who allow Jesus to work His way in them as they serve "On the Way."

The many church leaders within and beyond our Foursquare denomination, whose trust, encouragement and counsel has been a refining and edifying constant over the years.

Vincent and Connie Bird, our "Pop and Mom in the faith," who helped us through our early years of ministry and who still stand beside us during their latter years.

Darrell and Sharon Roberts and John and Linda Farmer, who first perceived God's call to tirelessly labor beside us in fulfilling the ministry given us, and who provide rock-like support and unselfish service always.

Our pastoral and supporting staff at the church, who lead the way with their lives in helping multitudes learn to live His life.

And for Janet Kemp, whose secretarial skills is only exceeded by her spiritual commitment manifested uniquely in a thousand ways, not the least of which was the typing of this manuscript.

". . . He has done great things," through these and countless others.

Jack Hayford

# Contents

# Introduction

*THE CHURCH ON THE WAY* is about a congregation with that name—"The Church On The Way" in Van Nuys, California.

It isn't a church growth testimony, but bears witness to the possibilities of growing people.

It tells a story, but it is more than a mere account. It teaches as it tells, for the unfolding of experiences becomes the discovery of biblical truth that has come alive in people.

I began to write a record for my own congregation—to help established members remember *why* we live as we do, and to teach new members *how* to move forward in even pace with God's purpose in our church.

But I was moved to change my style to write to a larger audience. To you who may become part of it, the approach of this book is simple. It is essentially a three-step pattern in all its parts:

1. I tell how the Holy Spirit taught me a principle of New Testament life, often in spite of my fumbling slowness.
2. I open the Scriptures to see how this principle is found in the root system of God's eternal Word.

3. Then I describe how one congregation seeks to live out that principle, trusting others will be helped to imagine how it will work for them.

"The Way" was the actual name of the first curriculum of study ever used in the Church, developed near the end of the first century. In *THE CHURCH ON THE WAY* we seek to show how the Lord of the Church has helped us get "on track" at points of *His* way that we had not understood. It has changed our hearts, our homes and, thereby, our church. Join us "on the way."

Your brother-in-grace,
Pastor Jack Hayford
Van Nuys, California

# Chapter 1

# CALLED TO A PEOPLE-CENTERED WORK

There were exactly two dozen people in the room, and six of them were members of my own family. Our group seemed even smaller for having been placed in a church sanctuary built to seat more than 200. Nevertheless, an air of excitement was present. It was Wednesday evening, March 8, 1969.

The roots of any renewal in the Church always begin with people; in this case with me, my wife and family. As Anna and I sat in the second row that night, our three older children (ages 12, 10 and 8) nestled beside us, with Anna holding our eleven-month-old baby in her arms.

Dr. N. M. Van Cleave, who supervised more than a hundred Foursquare churches in the southern California area, was officially introducing us as the new pastors of the Van Nuys congregation. It was a sort of homecoming for him and his wife, since they had once pastored this church decades before, in more fruitful years of its life. Mrs. Van Cleave had already introduced us privately to some of the dear elderly people who had gathered to greet us, for she knew most of them well from earlier years.

For only sixteen members to show up at a meeting like this might sound disappointing, but they were thrilled that "almost everyone" was present. In fact, a total of only eighteen members remained in this tiny congregation. But what they lacked in number and youthfulness they made up for in warmth and experience. They were loving people and they loved the Lord.

When I was introduced, instead of walking to the pulpit, I took a position in front of the first row of chairs and smiled.

"If no one minds," I began, "I would prefer to stand at floor level for what I'm going to say."

No one seemed to mind, nor do I suppose anyone really grasped my point at the time, but I had a reason for my positioning myself below the elevated platform. I was determined that for however long I would serve these people, I would function from a new level of understanding about pastoral service; and my position at their level was a kind of announcement.

None of us had the remotest dream of what was beginning with my few remarks that evening. I had simply consented to come here on a temporary assignment, feeling led by God to accept Dr. Van Cleave's invitation to assist this declining church. It was a "help-out-on-weekends-and-midweek-services" proposition, and the challenge it offered seemed exciting, but I did not expect we would do anything more than that for perhaps a year or so.

Nevertheless, in the months to come, God would shake me to the roots of my being, and I would learn church life at dimensions inconceivable to me that evening.

Still, I did have a sense of Christ's desire to renew His Church around the world; and however short my term of probable involvement here, I wanted to test those possibilities that the Word of God held forth.

So I asked that small handful of dear saints to read with me a passage from the New Testament:

Not that we are sufficient of ourselves to think any thing as of ourselves; but our sufficiency is of God; Who also hath made us able ministers of the new testament; not of the letter, but of the spirit: for the letter killeth, but the spirit giveth life.

(II Corinthians 3:5-6, KJV)

That evening's setting had been intended merely as the few moments for the new pastor to be introduced and to respond before we all retired to the basement fellowship hall for refreshments and personal greetings. But I felt I must make two things clear from the beginning. Thus, my opening remarks as pastor of the First Foursquare Church of Van Nuys, California, occupied only the next few minutes.

"I have read this passage," I said, "because it sets forth a principle that shall govern my thoughts and our life together for however long the Lord Jesus wills me to be your pastor."

Then I explained the context of the passage, and drew my listeners toward an observation that I had not understood myself until only a few months before: that this text focuses on the ministry of the believer. That is, every believer in Jesus Christ is promised a basic sufficiency for being and becoming what Jesus wants him or her to be. And what Jesus wants us to be is an expression of His life wherever we find ourselves.

No one seemed particularly impressed that night, nor did I really expect them to be. The reality and practicality of my words were not apparent at the moment. The proposition that "all of us are in this together" and that "I will be depending on you" sounds like the diplomatic, proper thing for any leader to say upon taking office.

But that was not my motive.

"I see us as becoming a truly 'ministry-minded' church," I explained. "The Lord Jesus Christ is our center. The Word of God is our base. The Holy Spirit, filling us to extend the servant life of Jesus outward—that's our objective. And praise God, this text assures us that He will make us sufficient to be and to become *able* ministers of this kind of New Testament life."

Then I added, "This will not be a pastor-centered ministry, but a people-centered ministry, all of us serving in Jesus' name."

In the first few weeks after that night, as I taught and preached, I began to develop some of the foundational concepts of New Testament ministry, stressing the fact that I would be learning together with the people along the way.

A bit of background may be useful to give perspective on what followed that beginning.

When I first accepted this pastorate, I was also serving as dean of students and member of the teaching faculty at LIFE Bible College in Los Angeles. I had been asked to take that position in 1965, following five years as National Youth Director for the Foursquare denomination.

LIFE was Anna's and my alma mater, where we both graduated in 1956, and entered the pastorate in Indiana—a ministry that also included much involvement in the regional Foursquare youth program.

The thirteen years from then until this evening in 1969 had been filled with responsibilities, studies and travels that would help equip us for what was about to happen. Through pastoral and faculty involvement, we had cultivated a grasp of the Word of God, with a strong background of Bible teaching and preaching experience. Besides this, our travels within our own denomination, as well as among many other groups, had given us a wide appreciation of the different streams of fellowship in the Church at large.

Furthermore, we had come in touch with the fact that by 1969, two streams of Holy Spirit enterprise in the Church around the world were converging rapidly: the classical Pentecostal stream and the spiritual flow now called the charismatic movement.

Anna and I both had been brought up in the Foursquare denomination, one of the older and more steadfast expressions of the Pentecostal revival that circled the earth in the early 1900s. Anna was born in North Platte, Nebraska, and from infancy had been involved in that community's Foursquare church. My own denominational background was more varied, quilted with various patches added every time our family moved during my childhood and adolescence.

My parents' spiritual birth occurred when I was only a year old. Jack and Dolores Hayford had responded to the message "Whosoever Will May Come," delivered by Pastor Watson R. Teaford at the Foursquare Church in Long Beach, California. A few weeks later, I was presented for infant dedication, according to the Scriptures, as my parents began to set their lives and home in biblical order.

In the coming years, I would receive my Bible training and grow spiritually in various denominations, but it would always be in a congregation where the Word of God was taught and where Jesus Christ was honored. My parents saw to that. I am indebted to God's providence to have years of background in the Presbyterian Church, the Society of Friends (Quakers), the Methodist Church and the Christian and Missionary Alliance. Intertwined with these experiences were periods of attendance in a Foursquare Church, when there was one near us.

With this combination of historic Protestant and Pentecostal church experience, we were also attuned closely to the sound of new showers of blessing that the Holy Spirit was raining upon the people of God everywhere. We understood the fear and resistance toward the charismatic movement that many of our fellow Pentecostals shared with leaders in denominations that were even older.

At times we had to admit that those fears were justified. Some charismatics often exhibited a distressing spiritual gullibility and love for sensationalism. It was disturbing to see evidences of people falling prey to the same excesses and exaggerations that have betrayed the blessing of God upon earlier revival seasons in Church history.

And so, to this new pastoral charge, I came seeing it as an especially challenging opportunity to walk with wisdom during a crucial time in the Church's life. On one hand, I carefully sought to avoid a "Pentecostalized" religious or denominationalistic prejudice; while on the other hand I sought to be wary of a reckless bent toward anti-institutional or hyper-spiritualistic habits developing among the charismatics.

We prized proven values rooted in the practice of the historic church, and also intended to realize the benefits of the renewal that were being seen in some places. So, from the perspective provided by our own background, we stepped into this pastorate, hoping for God's gracious workings.

Two capable young men quickly joined with me in the pursuit of what the Lord had for us in Van Nuys: Charles Shoemake, a fellow faculty member at LIFE Bible College, and Paul Charter, a senior student led by the Holy Spirit to partner with us. Our first Sunday at the church, both men with their wives, Ruby and Jerri, joined Anna and me.

Every Wednesday afternoon, Paul, Chuck and I met at the church for prayer and conversation concerning the work. Each of us had other occupations, but we felt the time well-spent, feeling keenly that God wanted to do something fresh in this old church—something that would require us to be sensitive, to seek His face, and to travel ways none of us had traveled before.

We felt as Joshua when he approached the river Jordan, heeding the divine caution, " . . . Ye have not passed this way heretofore" (Joshua 3:4). The promise of their future depended upon discretion in proceeding, and we sensed that same need for walking softly before God.

The pathway in *worship* that we taught the congregation; the transparency of *fellowship* that we sought to engender; and the *servant's attitude* that we urged the flock to assume—all these objectives were born from our prayer, sharing and learning together on those Wednesday afternoons.

We often laughed together. At other times we wept together. Slowly God was begetting a holy humanness and a human holiness among the three of us. We had no stilted images of each other, so our partnership was characterized by forthrightness and loving confrontation. Our relationships began to model something to the congregation.

Moreover, whenever we discovered places where human or church traditions were cropping up like weeds of religious habit choking simplicity from the church, we would examine those practices in the Word and with much prayer. We were persuaded that not all church traditions were invalid, and that church forms inherited from the past required cautious and prayerful consideration before being changed. We were bold enough to challenge history, but wise enough not to spurn its lessons, remembering the philosophic maxim: "Those who do not learn from history are destined to relive its errors."

The New Testament speaks both positively and negatively about tradition. A comparison of Matthew 15:2 with II Thessalonians 2:15 and 3:6, and Galatians 1:14 will show this. One passage warns against traditions that transgress God's own Word, while another urges, "Hold the traditions you have been taught."

We sought a fresh walk in the Spirit, but we recognized how easy it is to mistake novelty for newness. We also saw how easily pride can prompt an arrogant, anti-traditional stance, leading to a tireless quest to be "different." Sometimes older methods are better, and we were committed to avoiding "manpleasing," whether that man was a staid traditionalist or a rank newcomer to Spirit-filled living. We wanted to find Christ's mind for His Church, and to see the Holy Spirit work in our assembly according to the Father's Word, will and way.

We fumbled our way along at times, but hindsight seems to confirm that, as clumsy and unsensational as the slow way was, it established strong foundations for lasting ministry. Together we learned a thousand lessons—lessons in heart renewal through repentance; in humbling of self through open confession; and in Holy Spirit-begotten discovery through the Word.

Nine months went by, and our original handful of people became three handfuls. By December we were averaging about 65 in attendance, at which time God dealt with me, bringing me to a demanding level of commitment to this pastorate.

Until now my assignment had been a short-term deputation effort, commissioned by our district office as an attempt to help a diminishing parish survive. Then, three weeks before Christmas, the Lord deepened my awareness of His purpose for us. His orders came as a thought planted firmly in my mind: *You are to stay at this church.*

At first I shuddered at the thoughts provoked by this call. Only then did I realize that my liberty in this adventure in renewal had been based partially on the temporary nature of my assignment. Until then, in other words, I could always leave if the adventure didn't work out!

But now I was sensing God's commandment upon my life; and frankly, I was afraid. Although there had been a good beginning, I feared a permanent assignment to this little congregation. It might mean personal obscurity—pastoring a small Pentecostal church swallowed up in the megalopolis of southern California. Pride and fear I had never recognized now surfaced and had to be confronted. God had spoken, and I knew I had no truly viable options.

I had learned long before that God's call may seem bewildering, but that His ways always transcend ours. So, rather than wrestle with my reasonings or pursue my own presuppositions, I surrendered to that internal voice that had first summoned me as a boy, calling me to pastor. Now, after thirteen years of public ministry, I was looking forward to what appeared a bleak future in an obscure pastorate lost in Los Angeles' urban sprawl. I hoped God knew what He wanted to do with our lives, because I was not comfortable.

Nonetheless, when Christmas passed, we moved to the San Fernando Valley, nearer the church. We were *on the way* into

1970, but with no idea that these words would become syn-onomous with a marvelous doing of our heavenly Father.

# Chapter 2

# WHEN GOD SPEAKS

I have always felt a little uneasy with people who make spiritual life sound too "spiritualistic"—not that I object to biblical disciplines of holiness, or to a belief in the supernatural workings of God.

What I object to is the notion that holiness or a commitment to faith in God's supernatural power should produce bizarre practices or weird people. True spirituality and fuzzy mysticism are not related.

When the Holy Spirit fills a life, He does not neutralize the true humanity that God the Father created. Rather, He works to restore it to God's original, pre-sin-tainted function. The Holy Spirit's investiture in human flesh does not produce a "hybrid"—a being neither completely divine nor completely human.

Instead, His presence within us is intended to bring about a thoroughly spiritual and genuinely natural person. Jesus is the evidence that holiness and humanity can be blended successfully, beautifully and without affectation. And He will fill those He redeems today with the same Spirit who enabled His kind of life and His meaning in ministry.

That fullness, as we learn to respond to it in fearlessness and simplicity, will manifest itself in a uniting of sensitivity with spirituality, humanness with holiness, graciousness accompanied by glory.

The Scriptures note the divinely intended blend: "We have this treasure in earthen vessels" (II Corinthians 4:7, KJV). Here is God's peerless and pristine glory being invested in finite and fallible human treasure chests. Here is livable spirituality, far removed from the impossible pretense that some people attempt in an effort to be considered "spiritual."

The sort of supposed spirituality I reject is the ludicrous result seen in anyone who has confused the treasure with the chest. A false or contrived value of one's self will result in that person's taking himself too seriously, and will end up in his not taking God seriously enough. The effort at being holy in your own power exhausts your ability to draw on and rejoice in God's.

Thus, spirituality is neither fabricated nor dehumanizing; and in pressing this point, I am preparing to describe three occasions on which God spoke to me during the two years following our coming to Van Nuys.

I hope, by the preface I have just made, that these episodes will not appear either fanatical or presumptuous. With the words *God spoke to me*, I am making a specific statement predicated upon certain scriptural truths.

First, God speaks to everyone. He speaks to absolutely every human being by means of general and specific revelation. For example: the starry *heavens* bear testimony to His eternal power and Godhead (Psalm 19; Romans 1:20); our *conscience* is an inner voice of God (Romans 2:14-15); the *Bible* is the written Word of God (Romans 10:17); the historical evidence in His only begotten Son, *Jesus* of Nazareth, testifies to God (Acts 10:34-43); godly *relatives* influence some of us (II Timothy 1:5).

By these means, no human being is without some cases of direct address from the almighty God, to whom we will all have to give account. And since He has communicated so freely with us prior to our new birth, it is not surprising that

He continues to do so in even more personal ways once we become His children.

Secondly, God speaks to people in the church assembly. He speaks by direct impression, verbal or mental, as when the Holy Spirit prompts someone with a "word" from the Lord (I Kings 19:12-13; I Corinthians 14:1-5). Such subjective dealings with private hearts must always remain in alignment with established principles of His timeless Word; but make no mistake—God speaks intimately with His own.

And yet, in this case as I say, "God spoke to me," I am being even more specific than referring to general revelation or to private inner impressions. I reserve these words intentionally for the rare, special occasions when, in my spirit, I have had the Lord speak directly to me. I do not mean, "I felt impressed," or, "I sensed somehow."

Instead, I mean that at a given moment, almost always when I least expected it, the Lord spoke *words* to me. Those words have been so distinct that I am virtually able to say, "And I quote." Had anyone else been present, I do not believe they would have heard a sound. Nevertheless I am saying, "I *heard* the Lord speak."

I hasten to add that I do not believe God's "word" to anyone elevates him above others. God wants to commune and communicate with all who will seek Him in pure worship and holiness of heart (John 4:24; Jeremiah 29:11-13). He wants to lead us all, to direct and bless us, to show us the way we are to go.

To do this, He does not need to address us verbally each day, but there will be pivotal times in our lives when He will do exactly that. This is not the sole privilege of a select few, but neither is it a random action on God's part. He seeks those who seek Him, and He speaks when He has something distinct to say pertaining to that person's life and circumstance.

Sharing these "words" as I will, then, I think I am making it clear that I never believe that God's words to me must become binding on anyone else. Unless someone feels a harmony of heart and a witness through the Word, they need never do anything because I tell them what God has spoken to me. A word of God to my heart does not authorize me to manipulate anyone, and I reject "prophets" who use their "words" to dominate people.

The incidents I am sharing, however, generally bear witness to those who hear them. Also, if I do not describe these occasions when God spoke to me, I cannot give coherent explanation as to how God's grace began to pour upon "The Church On The Way."

They give a necessary dimension of understanding to three developments we have experienced in the life of our congregation: (1) marked and manifest growth; (2) a distinct sense of God's presence; (3) a sphere of influence incongruous to our size. Each of these blessings is related to something God said He would do; and He said these things to me in private moments of His own choosing.

The first time He spoke to me, He took me completely offguard. The words swept out of an apparent nowhere, landing on my consciousness: *You mustn't think too small.*

It was about six weeks after He had assigned me to remain in Van Nuys. I was driving along the Hollywood Freeway, drawing near the Sherman Way turnoff and home. Again His voice spoke: *You mustn't think too small, or you will get in My way.*

Instantly and intuitively, without reflection, I understood that the Lord was addressing my feeling of being consigned to an obscure, tiny pastorate.

Small thinking had never been characteristic of me, but in the breaking process of God's dealing with my heart over the last six weeks, I had become resigned to the supposition that the humbling, breaking process would mean lifelong obscurity and anonymity.

This resignation had not made me unhappy. In fact, I felt sincerely content, having surrendered the matter to the Father's will. God was speaking again, calling me to stretch open my heart and mind for something larger than I had supposed.

Then He spoke again, adding words that have become a dominant point of understanding for us: *You mustn't think too small, or you will get in My way; for I have set Myself to do a great work.*

With these words, the Holy Spirit flashed a vision into my mind, a scene snatched from the future, barely perceived but sufficient to show me that the largeness of the work would be in terms of property and buildings as well as people. It was not my own vision, just as those were not my own words; I knew the difference. God had given me a glimpse of enough to let me know He was committed to doing something sizable.

What happened after I heard those words was interesting, though not impressive by human measurements. The next Sunday our attendance nearly doubled. Without effort, program or emphasis, there were simply an additional 45 people present. It is a story in its own right how those people arrived together and at once, but the Lord had gotten my attention and demonstrated His word in a way that was intensely practical.

The following months, however, were not marked by extraordinary numerical growth. Instead, we grew in our spiritual perception. Prayer, praise and personal openness began to capture everyone's thinking that year. The new ones were aware that God was placing them into the working parts of something distinct in His purpose, and the older members were opening to fresh dimensions of a willingness to grow.

Together we began to focus on truth that shaped our individual and corporate ministry in *worship, fellowship* and *stewardship.* We began to grasp more thoroughly the following realities: (1) our ministry to the Lord in worship; (2) our ministry to one another in fellowship; (3) our ministry to the world, in our stewardship of what we had received as people of God's Kingdom.

It was the following autumn, as I sat in my study one day, that the Lord gave me what has become the slogan name for the Van Nuys Foursquare Church: "The Church On The Way."

The phrase *On The Way* focused on the fact that we are all moving forward in ministry—that is, a congregation available to be Jesus' life wherever we go and in whatever way He directs. Our address on Sherman Way lends a simpler point of reference to visitors and keeps the name from seeming supercilious, as though it were a claim to some kind of superiority. Above all else, it declares our message: Jesus! He is *the* Way.

It becomes clear, then, that with Him as primary and ultimate emphasis, anyone or any church can truly be "On The Way."

But our slogan name was not developed for promotionally clever reasons. It was born as a simple statement of ministry-mindedness, and I still feel this deeply. The name is meaningless without that commitment; and only people willing to grow can properly say, "I'm part of 'The Church On The Way.'" Availability to the Holy Spirit's work, making the serving life of Jesus Christ alive and real through us, is our primary objective—not cultivating a label or a slogan.

The congregation grew in understanding and practice in several ways during those months: first, in worship and in a willingness to communicate with one another. Many churches succumb to social pressures to conform their worship patterns and interpersonal communication to the unwritten yet real demands of our culture. Consequently, open and forthright praise is suppressed as unseemly and unsophisticated.

Understandably, many fear that if open, expressive worship is sustained for any length of time, it will give rise to fanatical or raucous behavior. A stereotype of wild-eyed "holy roller-ism," or some other strain of offbeat emotionalism or cultishness, has introduced a controlling fear into today's church life.

To praise God demonstrably is, many suppose, to risk being ostracized as unrespectable, to have abandoned good sense.

But when a people commit themselves to worship according to scriptural guidelines, and if their leaders are faithful to praise God openly, at length, beautifully and biblically, God is more interested in our expressing our worship than He is in the opinions of society regarding our forms.

The first Sunday morning I ever led the members of the congregation into direct and extended communication with one another, as part of the service itself, was the same day I introduced the slogan name, "The Church On The Way." I told them we were instituting a practice that would require a new willingness and openness. It would be a time of interaction and prayer in small circles, and would become a frequent part of our gatherings.

"Ministrytime," the general term we use for that segment in many of our services, was a stretching point for newcomers to the church. But, interestingly, the people who had the most difficulty with it were those with the longest history of traditional church life. The newborn in the Family didn't think it strange; rather, those whose background had accustomed them to non-participative habits in public worship, who often had to overcome a sort of brittleness resulting from their past experience.

The most beautiful thing about our prayer circles was that they established a springboard for ministry. They gave each of us practice at listening to others, then finding the Holy Spirit's help to frame prayers appropriate to the needs discussed.

In this setting, too, the Lord took opportunity to give people impressions, Scripture passages and ideas that also spoke to the needs of the people. After all, we began to learn, if we couldn't do this sort of thing in the company of brothers and sisters, we certainly weren't likely to do so when we were out where others we met needed His life happening through us.

So, the growth to this time was essentially in understanding and practice. Aside from that one-time surge at the beginning of the year, when we nearly doubled, the attendance held constant during the whole of 1970. After nearly two years, our Sunday morning congregation numbered about 100.

But God was about to speak again.

# Chapter 3

# THE GIFT OF HIS GLORY

It was the first Saturday of 1971, and I had spent the afternoon in my office, studying and finalizing my message for the next day's service. Folding my completed notes into my Bible, I turned off the desk light and left the office, walking into the sanctuary and down the aisle to set the thermostat located on the front wall beside the prayer room door.

It was a clear, crisp, sunshiny day—perfect southern California wintertime weather, as generally characterizes the globally televised Rose Bowl game that had taken place the day before. But the nights are frosty, and I set the thermostat so that the sanctuary would be comfortable for the congregation gathered the next morning.

The wall clock read 4:30. I felt pleased that I was completely prepared for the morrow and en route home, early for dinner without Anna's having to call. I set the dial at seventy-two degrees, and turned to leave the room. But then I paused, standing bewildered beside the piano.

The room was filled with a silvery mist.

The late afternoon sun slanted through the stained-glass windows, adding to the beauty of the sight before me; but there was no natural explanation for what I was seeing. The mist had not been there a moment before. My mind probed for an answer: "This isn't dust . . . smog . . . is it?"

The real answer preceded the question, for in my heart I knew better. It was crystal-clear outside; this wasn't smog. And there was no earthly dust that had the glowing quality that this mist possessed as it filled the whole room, even where the sunlight wasn't shining.

*I know what it is*, I thought to myself. But in fact, I was hesitant to admit it.

*Test it out first*, my reason countered. *If it's the Lord, it will stand closer scrutiny.*

I stepped into the prayer room. No mist there. I rubbed my eyes before stepping back into the sanctuary. *If it's just me, that will take care of it.*

But as I scanned the sanctuary again, it was evident that the unusual mistiness was still present.

I was neither startled nor frightened, for I felt in my spirit that I *did* know what I was seeing. I was just reticent to claim as much to myself.

You see, I had observed this sort of thing once before, about a year earlier. I had just lifted my eyes from prayer with one of the students at the college after a counseling session in my office there. The same kind of mist had filled the room.

Neither of us spoke at first. Then I ventured a gesture and inquired, "Do you—?"

The student nodded affirmatively. We sat for about fifteen seconds, and then the mist gradually disappeared, as though dialed down by a rheostat.

"And now it's gone," I observed aloud, and the student confirmed as much.

We had each heard of the *shekinah*, the radiant, visible glory of God of which the Bible speaks. But seeing it—for that was our mutual understanding and conviction—was something new for us both.

Now I was witnessing it again, but two things were significantly different: no one was with me to confirm the vision, and I had not been at prayer, as on the other occasion. I felt a peculiar sense of wonder—why this display? Strangely enough, I was also concerned about who could confirm that I wasn't just seeing things.

Then the Lord spoke: *It is what you think it is.*

The words struck me as moving and humorous at the same moment. The almighty God of the universe saw me worrying about a confirming witness and condescended to be that witness Himself. It was as though God were saying, "I see it too, Jack." That was the humorous part.

What moved me deeply were the words that followed: *I have given My glory to dwell in this place."*

I stood, watching silently; and moments later the scene returned to the ordinariness of mere sunlight in the room.

Strangely, I felt inclined to do nothing unusual. I remember thinking, "Thank You, Lord," but otherwise I was relatively unresponsive. I didn't fall down in worship. I didn't feel I should take my shoes off. I didn't sense any dominant emotion of any kind. I knew only that I had seen what I had seen, and heard what I had heard. I went on home and said nothing of the vision to anyone for some time.

But the implications of that afternoon were soon to be realized. Looking back, I would realize it was clearly a moment of enormous consequence.

The next day, instead of the usual hundred or so in attendance, there were more than 160 worshipers in the morning service. There had been no special emphasis, no promotional campaign, no advertising, nothing—except that the day before God had said He was giving a gift.

It was years before I shared publicly the story of that afternoon, because I realized it could be sorely misunderstood. But from that day there has been an extraordinary ongoing work of grace among us. Lives have been changed, bodies healed, homes rescued, people delivered, truth perceived, love outpoured.

And our numerical growth has been remarkable, from the few saints prior to that second day of 1971, until this writing in

1982, when more than 4,300 gather each Sunday morning. Moreover, this numbers only one service, the Sunday morning gathering, and does not reflect the additional thousands of people being helped by other ministries and services of the church.

Of course, many other churches have grown far larger, but the figures in our records demonstrate that something distinguishable has happened.

Trained leaders efficient in church work tend to disbelieve the words that follow here, but they are true: We have done nothing to promote, produce or program for this growth. Everything we do that might be called a "program" is simply a response to what God has done and is doing. We do our best to keep pace with *His* work—not try to get Him to endorse ours.

Thus, without any notable plan, other than seeking to be faithful to those principles the Holy Spirit has made alive in our hearts, "The Church On The Way" has grown; but His glory gift was the key to this release.

Several lessons have flowed out of this, which deserve to be understood by all who would live within the realm of God's glory, a privilege He desires for all His people.

The first lesson is that God does desire to manifest His glory among His people.

Arise, shine; for thy light is come, and the glory of the Lord is risen upon thee. For, behold, the darkness shall cover the earth, and gross darkness the people: but the Lord shall arise upon thee, and his glory shall be seen upon thee.

(Isaiah 60:1-2, KJV)

This was not my understanding, from my earliest memory. I had always thought God to be jealous about His glory, and unwilling to allow anyone else to share in it. It was only at the prompting of this experience that I searched the Scriptures for the oft-quoted words, "My glory will I not give to another."

If the Word of God said that, and if, on the other hand, my experience that day contradicted it—for God had said, "I have given My glory to dwell in this place"—then I would renounce my experience and take hold of the eternal Word engraved in the Scriptures.

The prophecy of Isaiah, however, in which God emphasizes His refusal to share His glory with another, defines clearly who "another" is:

I am the Lord; that is my name: and my glory will I not give to another, neither my praise to graven images.

(Isaiah 42:8, KJV)

God denies the sharing of His excellency, majesty and glory with other gods, or any being that boasts itself against Him.

In distinct contrast Jesus said, concerning the Father's own people who honor His Messiah and who have received His witness:

And the glory which thou gavest me I have given them; that they may be one, even as we are one . . . .

(John 17:22, KJV)

Jesus Himself, who embodied the fullness of God's glory, has transmitted that glory unto His Church, "which is his body, the fullness of him that filleth all in all" (Ephesians 1:23).

The second lesson we learned from that day is that His glory attends those who worship Him in *His* way. The Scriptures show that God manifested His glory in a visible sense when His order of worship was established and honored among His people. With the completion of the Tabernacle in Moses' time we read:

And he reared up the court round about the tabernacle and the altar, and set up the hanging of the court gate. So Moses finished the work. Then a cloud covered the tent of the congregation, and the glory of the Lord filled the tabernacle. And Moses was not able to enter into the tent of the congregation, because the cloud abode thereon, and the glory of the Lord filled the tabernacle.

(Exodus 40:33-35, KJV)

Similarly, in Solomon's time, with the completion and dedication of the Temple, the Scriptures record:

It came even to pass, as the trumpeters and singers were as one, to make one sound to be heard in praising and thanking the Lord; and when they lifted up their voice with the trumpets and cymbals and instruments of music, and praised the Lord, saying, For he is good; for his mercy endureth forever: that then the house was filled with a cloud, even the house of the Lord; So that the priests could not stand to minister by reason of the cloud: for the glory of the Lord had filled the house of God.

(II Chronicles 5:13-14, KJV)

Ordered worship introduces the glorious order of the Eternal One. "I will glorify the house of my glory," the Lord declares, and then adds: "I will make the place of my feet glorious" (Isaiah 60:7, 13, KJV).

In short, where people worship God according to His Word, He will respond with a distinct working of His presence, and the rule of His glorious Kingdom comes in all its liberating power. That is why wherever people honor the Word of God, exalt the Son of God and give place to the Spirit of God, distinct and marvelous blessing pours forth.

All this is not the heritage of a denomination, or even of those of a particular doctrinal stripe. It is not the portion of the charismatic as opposed to the noncharismatic, nor of the Protestant as opposed to the Catholic. It is the increasing portion of any congregation that pursues a pathway of humility before God's throne, His Word, His Son and His Spirit. God comes there to abide.

Whether or not the vision is visible, as was my experience, God may be distinctly present. People can recognize it and they will gather there, for I believe most of mankind longs intuitively for this fulfillment.

The absence of God's glory characterizes fallen man, whether in the case of Adam and Eve, stripped of glory when sin entered the race, or in our own case, as members of that race who have "come short of the glory of God" (Romans 3:23). The searching of the human heart for completion is ultimately fulfilled only in the presence of that glory.

The third lesson we learned is that God's glory in the midst of a people may be lost. It will be diminished to whatever degree the will of the flesh and the pride of human hearts persist in their own way, regenerated though the individuals may be.

After Samson's indulgence and surrender to Delilah's connivings, we read:

> And she said, The Philistines be upon thee, Samson. And he awoke out of his sleep, and said, I will go out as at other times before, and shake myself. And he wist not that the Lord was departed from him.
>
> (Judges 16:20, KJV)

The gift of God's unique blessing upon Samson was contingent upon his continuing in his vow to walk God's ways. His tragedy was not only that he lost that distinctive presence of God; but worse, that he didn't even recognize it was gone until he was crippled at the hands of his enemy.

Over the years the Holy Spirit has sharply reproved our congregation on a number of occasions. Worship may become habitual and tinny, rather than wholehearted and vibrant. Incredibly, hearts can become as hardened *to* the presence of God as they can be *against* it. A church can be deceived into thinking that its growth verifies the congregation's righteousness.

That is a delusion. Any well-managed business can grow, with or without God. Samson said, "I will shake myself as at other times," and in his words we hear the echo of a thousand religious organizations that have learned the moves to make in order to make things happen "as at other times."

The challenge before us is to walk before God in purity and wholeheartedness—to hospitably entertain His glory through genuine worship from hearts that truly love and obey Him.

God's glory and His grace are two different matters. His grace is offered to sinners. His glory is offered to those willing to walk in His way.

"Worship the Lord in the beauty of holiness," the Scriptures enjoin time and again; and those who have tasted the *beauty* of holiness have no question what that phrase means. It is the loveliness of His glory—the radiance of His presence.

I want to enjoy that gift through all my life, in all of this church, and unto all eternity.

# Chapter 4

# BREAKING OUT OF POVERTY

Poverty is more than not having; it is a spirit that is always *fearful* of not having. That fear affects the entire human race, being so massive a force that even though a person has much, he still tends to think it will never be enough.

We are born crying out with clutching fingers grasping for what we want. Although mind and body develop, and tears and tantrums come under reasonable control, only a work of grace can remove our insatiable sense of needing to get, to have, and to keep for ourselves.

I did not recognize how this mentality had characterized my own pastoral work and church leadership. Whatever I did notice, I would never have defined as selfishness, for the self-protectiveness begotten by the spirit of poverty is usually different from greediness. But even though it is not as hateful as stinginess, it can bind us as badly. I was to discover how much more motivated I was to get than to give, but the trait had become well-masked in peculiar and seemingly spiritual ways.

In my first pastorate, for example, I did door-to-door work, sincerely believing I was pursuing a Christ-honoring search for the unchurched. God was gracious to allow us to see a few souls brought to His Son through those efforts, but I realize now I was far more deeply concerned about how my pastorate

would grow than I was truly moved with compassion as Jesus
was:

> But when he saw the multitudes, he was moved with compassion
> on them, because they fainted, and were scattered abroad, as sheep
> having no shepherd.
>
> (Matthew 9:36, KJV)

Another trait of that fear manifested when visitors came to a
service. I was tempted to cater to them at the expense of
forthrightness. I might have called it diplomacy, but it was in
fact dishonesty, motivated by the fear of not being able to "get
a crowd" unless I used humanized methods. Experience had
taught me how, by the casual modification of some remarks, I
could attempt to provide an image of the church that might
persuade a visitor's continued attendance.

But I learned that promotional banter, slick presentations
and glad-handed superficiality may gain someone's membership, but will never cultivate people of strong character and
true commitment.

The evidence of such poverty-mindedness—the fear of not
*getting*—eventually surfaced in my thought patterns and terminology.

One Sunday shortly after we came to Van Nuys, a family of
five visited our morning worship. As a result of information I
gained while conversing with them following the service, I
remarked to Anna on the way home, "It sure would be nice to
get them into the church. We could use a family like that."

It was then that the Holy Spirit helped me to hear myself:
*Get. Use.* I was smitten with shameful awareness, and for
several days following I reflected on what seemed like a hundred behaviorial patterns undergirded by a spirit that was
fundamentally wrong.

Poverty—the fear of not getting, of not having—had to go.
Faulty material in the foundation must be removed at any cost.
So I submitted to God's Spirit. There could be no true building

of the Church of Jesus Christ by my scheming, promoting personnel work, or any concern preoccupied with *getting*. You can't partner with Christ in His building of the Church if you have clutching hands.

And therein lay a further discovery. My basic fault was my failure to perceive that Jesus is not only the Church's Foundation; He is also its Architect and Builder. "I will build My Church," He announced on a mountainside in Galilee long ago. Now those words were being engraved on my soul.

When I repented, God released a flow of love and giving from me that would eventually take over the congregation. We would come to realize and live in the awareness that the Church's reason for being is to give away and to serve; to lay down its life and watch the Lord Jesus work resurrection miracles over and over.

A refining point of discovery in this realm occurred when the Lord spoke to me again only two months after I saw God's glory in the sanctuary. This message helped me discover several basic principles about Christ and His Church, and it included a perspective on finances that began the liberation process in me and the leaders within our congregation.

It was past one o'clock in the morning as I sat in our living room rocking chair, my bathrobe wrapped around me against the late-night chill. As I waited in prayer, I paused at one point in my intercession, and with crystal clarity the Lord spoke. His question seemed very peculiar to me.

*You don't believe you're in My will, do you?*

I couldn't have agreed less or been puzzled more. I *did* believe I was in His will, yet He was suggesting that I didn't—not really. I kept my mouth shut and my mind open.

*Do you believe you are to be pastoring?*

I nodded affirmatively, as though He were seated across from my chair.

*Do you believe you are to pastor in Van Nuys?*

Again I affirmed as much.

*Do you believe you are to pastor the Van Nuys Foursquare Church?*

Of course I did! What kind of quiz was this? God had suggested I didn't believe I was in His will, and everything He asked I was affirming.

And then came His felling thrust, one that left me in complete disarray:

*You believe that being in the Foursquare denomination is your own idea.*

My mind reeled. A dozen different streams of thought converged at once. For the next several moments I attempted to sort them out.

It was true, although I had never perceived it in those terms. I *was* in the Foursquare denomination. I wasn't unhappy about it either, not thinking of leaving for another group or an independent posture.

But, upon analysis, I realized I *did* believe "being Foursquare" was my own decision. I had come to a Foursquare Bible College for training years before, and the natural flow of events seemed to draw me into that fellowship.

Sure. I guess I *did* think it was a matter of natural choice. I mean, after all, isn't being in a particular denomination anyone's own decision? Surely God doesn't care which you choose. I mean, He's basically indifferent to the whole ecclesiastical hodge-podge, and only actually cares about people, not church groups, and . . . .

And now my thoughts were being interrupted by a revelation from God's heart to mine. He was showing me that I didn't truly believe it was His will for me to be in the Foursquare Church; and suddenly I saw three things.

First, I saw the ludicrous nature of the supposition that I could claim to be in God's will pastoring the Van Nuys Foursquare Church if the "Foursquare" part was immaterial. It was an inseparable proposition, the significance of which had been wholly imperceptible to me until that moment.

The second thing I saw was that God loves denominations.

Please notice, I did not say God loves *denominationalism.* Denominationalism is seen in the smallness, divisiveness and sniping that proceed from the sectarian love of a denomination for its own sake. That mindset lacks God's endorsement completely.

Such "ism" may be embraced by independents or denominations and called "a kindred spirit." But the painful truth is that often the spirit of supposed unity is actually a sectarian party spirit, and a false order of joy derived through self-congratulation over one's own doctrinal purity, personal piety, ecclesiastical accomplishment or public recognition. This separation is an "ism," and needs to be seen as such.

Yet God *does* love denominations, because God loves people. The true essence of a denomination is that it is a distinct family group of people within the larger family of our Father, "of whom the whole family in heaven and earth is named" (Ephesians 3:15, KJV). Just as Israel had tribes with family groups within those tribes, yet they were all one people, so the Church is not outside of the divine will where denominations exist.

What transgresses God's will is the absence of love, and the pride that supposes any of us has a corner on truth. We need to see that our denomination of apple trees is only part of the ranch, and that trees of oranges, apricots, peaches and even *lemons* might be as fruitful in His eyes as our own self-approved corner of the field.

Furthermore, it jarred me to see that God might have some isolated trees outside the orchards, as a professional landscaper might have for ornamentation. In other words, what appeared to me to be "independent" churches may have a place in His plan, too.

The danger of sectarian smallness can grip an independent pastor, of course, as readily as it could grip me as a denominational pastor. We were all vulnerable to the pride that carries us toward self-assertion and self-authentication, prying us

apart from each other, binding us in the ridigity of loveless-
ness.

The third revelation flashing into my awareness in that
midnight moment was that God was calling me to understand
my obligation to participate in the principles of my denomination's mode of operation.

I am not saying that God told me my denomination was
right in all its processes and procedures. While I presume all
of us seek to be as precisely structured to New Testament
church methods as possible, we would all do well to acknowledge honestly that there isn't enough information in the Scriptures to instruct us conclusively in our own formation of
ecclesiastical structures.

Any debate as to whether the congregational, episcopal or
presbyterian form of church government is most righteous, or
as to whether deacons or elders ought to lead the church, or as
to whether a given congregation ought to use literature from
the presses of its denomination exclusively, or as to which
parachurch organizations are justified and which are not—all
this debate is so much rhetorical rummaging.

God could not care less about our self-justifying arguments.
The real issue is this: Do you function in a spirit of submission
and loving self-giving in the circle of fellowship where He has
placed you?

That night the issue was solved for me, because I was *not*
functioning in that way. It was not as though I was making
trouble or arguing or sowing discord, because I wasn't.
Rather, my unwillingness to submit showed up in the partial
participation I gave toward the financial program of my denomination.

Nor was I alone in this limited pattern of cooperation. I had
learned it from the majority of pastors in our fellowship. Let
me explain.

Our denomination funds its mission by a monthly "extension tithe." This guideline calls for each participating church

to send ten percent of its general tithes and offerings each month to the regional office of the denomination. (Missionary offerings and specially designated funds, such as building or development gifts, are exempt from the extension tithe.)

Although the corporate bylaws of the denomination show this tithe to be a required point of participation, the matter has come to depend over the years on the leadership of each local pastor. Thus, the extension tithe has become a voluntary matter, and I never heard of a pastor or congregation being disciplined for not participating in the program.

The irony of our situation was that, at that time, we were sending a "token tithe" of $100 per month to our regional office when our church's monthly income was about $2,500. This tokenism was not uncommon with many Foursquare congregations, but when I look back, I marvel at how I rationalized this practice.

What a ridiculous term—"token tithe." To be sure! Imagine Abraham saying to Melchizedek, "You know, sir, the plunder from this victory is so great that it seems unreasonable to give you a full tenth. If you please, I think I'll simply give you this *token*, which I think you'll agree is quite sizable enough."

It's sadly laughable; for the Bible says that Abraham, in whose footsteps of faith the New Testament tells us all to walk (Romans 4:12-16), "gave him tithes of *all*" (Genesis 14:20, italics added).

I was beginning to realize that my pastoral leadership would determine the mood of the whole congregation. First, the spirit of poverty was dictating a withheld tithe; and that fear of not having enough—the fear of giving more than we had to—had to be broken. Further, the spirit of submission in all of our congregation could be extended or hindered by my response.

I am convinced that the conflicts within many congregations are simply the sad projection of the pastor's own lack of submission to God's will in some part of his own life. Psalm 133, which celebrates the blessedness of brethren dwelling in unity, says that unity is "like the precious ointment upon the head, that ran down upon the beard, even Aaron's beard: that went down to the skirts of his garments" (vv. 1-2, KJV).

*Unity flows down from the head,* and I cannot expect any more unity, love or submittedness in my congregation than I exhibit in the way I obey God; in the way I lead my household in love and peace; and in the way I submit to those whom God has placed over me in government, be it civil or ecclesiastical.

God was not endorsing my denomination's financial plan above any other, but He was teaching me that the imperfection in *all* human government can be compensated for only by His grace. That grace flows in its richest dimensions only when those within a group submit graciously and lovingly to the methods of operation by which that particular group has chosen to govern itself. It is only wisdom to perceive that His government is in spirit and truth, and is not perfected in the hands of legalists, but in the hearts of free and loving people.

As a result of this late-night encounter with the Lord, I asked the men of our church council to meet with me. I told them I believed we should bring our church's extension tithe to a consistent tenth, and I explained why. Relating God's dealing with me on this matter, I went on to explain.

Our particular denomination, I observed, took the principle of the extension tithe from Numbers 18:26, in which the Lord told Moses to require the Levites to offer a tithe of the tithes they received to Him. (See also Nehemiah 10:38.)

A New Testament principle was also at stake:

Let every soul be subject unto the higher powers. For there is no power but of God: the powers that be are ordained of God. Whosoever therefore resisteth the power, resisteth the ordinance of God.

(Romans 13:1-2, KJV)

When I expressed how deeply it appeared to me that God was summoning us to manifest our submission to those authorities that He had placed over us in family association, the brothers consented heartily. We paid our tithe, retroactive to the preceding month, and from that date we have given it as a faithful minimum.

That sum, in the current year, will total over one-third of a million dollars, and we delight in the knowledge that those monies are used by our denominational leaders, among other needful things, to help birth many new congregations in different parts of the nation, and to strengthen weak churches unto health.

With that decision, it was as though a lid came off. An entirely new viewpoint captured my mind, and the liberty it brought began to swell within the hearts of those in the congregation. While every congregation has its own basic financial needs to tend to, we began to realize that our largest responsibility was to be available prayerfully and unselfishly to *give*. The giving was more than merely monetary. It affected other attitudes of selfishness we had failed to recognize.

When people felt they were to leave our church to go to another, for example, instead of forcing them to slip out the side door secretively, as it were, we began to teach people a fearlessness in this regard. Members of the congregation became free to express to the pastor or elders their sense of God's direction when they felt drawn to another assembly.

We refused to attempt to dissuade them. We began to take delight in sending people forth with our blessing, allowing them to go with a positive sense of God's purpose and ministry for them. Our will to function in this spirit was no less gracious when folks expressed their plans to attend a congregation of another denomination.

And, as we served and gave more and more, doors of opportunity opened more and more, making room for God to show His hand of power and provision through us.

This is no magic wand principle. Learning to give does not preempt recurrent lessons in faith or periodic confrontations again with the fearful spirit of poverty.

And I wholly reject the popularized notion that to break poverty is to enter into a self-gratifying wealth. Without recognizing it, some American Bible teachers have developed an unbiblical, humanistic theology of abundance that is, in actuality, nothing more than an attempt to justify North American acquisitiveness and affluence. This attempt to give license to selfishness washes out in the face of life's realities being lived by most people in the rest of the world.

Neither will it hold water when character-testing trials confront believers in this land. I do affirm that God wants us all to abound, and the Bible does teach that poverty is a broken curse; but the abundance He wants to lavish upon us—upon His Church—is not for our own aggrandizement. It is for our service and ministry to the rest of His Body and to the world.

Just as the breaking of poverty does not argue for a superficial justification of affluence, neither does it result from a mismanaged giveaway philosophy. Some idealists have proposed that everyone in the Church should give away everything. They propose that we be "like the New Testament church," and they quote from the book of Acts to underscore their supposedly righteous program of "community"—everybody having the same things.

But Acts 4:32-5:11 illustrates a responsible *sharing in need*, not an equalizing of resources. God does bless people who learn diligence, order and management, and there is no guilt to be associated with the possession of large resources. But the possession of much is not the essence of freedom from poverty. The essence of this freedom is freedom from the need to get; freedom from the need to be in control; freedom from the need to protect yourself compulsively at every turn.

So it was that we began to realize the beginning of freedom from the yoke of poverty. Monies tithed were discovered to "cost" us nothing; for God's blessing, which cannot be bought, is released through this obedience. People released in faith to serve elsewhere went away with their relationship to us intact, and the Holy Spirit was freed to expand us because of our interest in Christ's *whole* Church, rather than a preoccupation with only our own.

People sent are given, not lost. Monies sent or expended are directed or invested, not "spent," for you cannot actually spend what comes from God's hand as a gift to you. "All that we have comes from Him and we give it out of His hand" (I Chronicles 29:14, Dutch translation).

# Chapter 5

# THE PRIORITY IN MINISTRY

We came to Van Nuys chiefly to equip believers to minister the life and the love of Christ with grace and ability.

By pure scriptural assignment, church leaders are commissioned to serve this objective, and dare not accept a hierarchical role as a spiritual "professional." The Bible says Jesus has given leaders to His Church to develop *every* believer to do the work of ministry and to upbuild the Church:

And he gave some, apostles; and some, prophets; and some, evangelists; and some, pastors and teachers; for the perfecting of the saints, for the work of the ministry, for the edifying of the body of Christ.

(Ephesians 4:11-12, KJV)

It took me a long time to understand this concept; and the Holy Spirit was remarkably patient in teaching me.

In 1967 one of the older students in the college came to me, filled with excitement. As he spoke, I learned. He expressed his eagerness to begin his public ministry so that he could be an instrument "in developing the capacity of *every* member of the Body for ministry."

I sensed his enthusiasm, but still listened unresponsively. The Spirit was telling me that the young man had struck a vein of truth, but for the life of me, I couldn't absorb it. As he left my office, I assured him of my encouragement as he moved on toward graduation. Yet somehow, deep inside, I knew something had been related to me that transcended my spiritual grasp.

I finished with that encounter feeling that a key to how the Church was to fulfill its calling had been taught to me—and by a student of mine at that! But I did not really grasp it, not at all. Embarrassing.

A year later, since I was professor of evangelism at the college, I was asked by our denomination's leadership to represent them at a conference on evangelism being held by another denomination. There, this concept was presented again:

*The ministry of the Church is to be extended through every member of the Body, assisted and released by pastoral and other leadership.*

The Holy Spirit was beginning to get through to me!

The unusual outline of the conference helped jar me to full attention. The first speaker startled me with a new idea: that evangelism begins with worship. The second speaker showed that, following the integrated worship, the Church must become an integrated fellowship. Only then, to my amazement, was the topic of direct outreach—evangelism—finally broached.

At once, it all fit together for me: The subjects, or the principals, of ministry are the laity, and the sequence, or the priority, of ministry is that *evangelism follows worship and fellowship.* Evangelism, I now was able to see, was the byproduct of spiritual life flowing from a healthy Body nourished through worship and fellowship.

My spirit witnessed to the truth, but my mind recoiled in doubt. I looked around me for confirming evidence in the response of others there. But most pastors present were apparently not on the same wavelength. They seemed to be as I had been during that conversation in my office a year before: chained to traditional ideas about the pastor's role and about the church's program of evangelism.

The idea that evangelism should be performed primarily by laymen and that the pathway to evangelism began with the worship and fellowship of the Church were well outside their range of acceptance, if not beyond their imagination. Until this moment, it had been beyond mine, too.

Worship first? Mysticism! The people as the ministers? Anarchy!

If it were not for the fact that in 1968 I was not myself pastoring, I'm not sure I would have seen it. Even if I had seen it, I might not have been receptive to the idea.

I viewed worship more as a periodic activity than a key to the release of the Church's power. As for the idea of ministry being given to the laity—well, frankly, it's threatening to think your field of expertise might actually be anyone's (everyone's?) domain. It seemed tantamount to saying that the way to build a house is to give tools to every child in the neighborhood and turn them loose on a woodpile.

But as I spent time studying the Word of God, the Holy Spirit helped me to absorb these concepts and see how they could be applied.

First, I saw that every member of the Body has the potential to be—and should be fed and led toward functioning as—a fully equipped agent of Jesus Christ, as His minister. I saw that goal as a reachable one, predicated upon two propositions:
1. No one's ministry can mature unless it is taught, trained and lovingly served.
2. Christ has given apostles, prophets, evangelists and pastor-teachers to do that task.

The picture was clearing up. This was not a threat to pastoral leadership, but a demanding, self-giving assignment. A person's years of study at college and seminary would not be wasted because of the sudden preempting of need for trained pastors or church leaders by a magically enlightened laity. The leaders were the key to the laity's release in ministry—in fact, absolutely necessary to it. But in spirit the leader would have to make a commitment.

As I reflected on this, it came down to one question: Would I be willing to do my job—train the congregation for the work of the ministry—if it meant I might end up out of work? Perhaps they could sustain the ongoing ministry of the church without me. Was I ready for that?

It may sound strange or dumb, but I honestly wondered about that issue. I decided for an affirmative answer. And I remember telling Anna, "Honey, if equipping people to minister really works, in a couple of years I could be selling shoes."

I meant it. I intended to pursue the vision whatever it would cost.

But I wasn't prepared for two things that happened—two things that removed my availability to the shoe industry.

First, I wasn't prepared for the growth we enjoyed. I had thought church growth came through programs, promotion, goalsetting and busywork. One had to pray, preach and read the Bible, too, I felt, but the key was *working at it*—especially on programs and publicity.

Now I was beginning to discover another kind of growth. It was the growth of people gaining God's viewpoint on themselves, on His love for them, and on His purpose for their lives. The Word of God and the love of God were growing big people, the kind of people who enlarge everything around them.

The church began to grow—not all at once, but it did grow. And I began to discover that although the maturing ones did not need me as much as they once had, a new crop of people was rising who *did* need me. They were the babes in Christ, the newcomers into the congregation, the adolescents turning the corner into college/career years and early adult maturity. All of them needed what I had to give.

The other thing I wasn't prepared for was how much the new ministers—the laity—came to love us. As they grew, some of the people didn't actually need Anna and me any longer, having themselves come to a point of stability, maturity and beginning ministry. Yet they loved us. It was a new dimension of love, a deep, committed quality that people began showering on us. They realized we had poured something of our lives into theirs, and they loved us.

With years of this behind us now, incredibly, they still don't tire of us as we all keep growing, "from glory to glory, even as by the Spirit of the Lord" (II Corinthians 3:18, KJV).

The leadership of the Body does require trained people, of course. It is not a compromise to tradition or carnal habit that a congregation has a salaried staff of people giving their full time to assisting the congregation along in the will and way of God's Word and purpose.

While I was on study leave recently, Anna and I visited the Presbyterian Church in Carmel, California. The sign beside the church office read:

Ministers:    *Every Member*
Assistants:   (the pastoral staff was listed here)

In that same spirit we had made our chief objective the development of each person as a minister. Consequently, the question of how to do that had become the most pressing item on our agenda.

Three things helped me work out the answer: (1) the outline given at the conference I mentioned; fitted to (2) an understanding I had received years before; and joined with (3) an insight gained while teaching at the college.

At this same conference I was given an outline for the Church's ministry as prescribed by the Scriptures. It was summarized under three headings: *Ministry to the Lord; Ministry to the Saints;* and *Ministry to the World.* The first involves the worship of the congregation; the second, their fellowship as brothers and sisters in Christ; and the third, evangelism—reaching those who do not know life in the Son of God.

As these were discussed, emphasis was made on their essential order, if evangelism was to result effectively and according to the Word. So in this chapter, as well as in the next, I'd like to take each of these headings in turn.


## Ministry to the Lord

I had not understood why worship was at the top of the list. In my mind, it logically followed evangelism. After all, I assumed, "We have to get them saved first. We can't prioritize the humming of hymns while the world goes to hell, can we?"

Without my realizing it, my whole experience in the milieu of evangelical Christianity had evolved a philosophy that made evangelism the god of the church. The components of true worship had been laid at the shrine of soul-saving.

All *sacrifice* was for evangelism of the world.
All *surrender* was for the salvation of souls.
All *ministry* was to reach the lost.
All *effort* and *planning* was to get people saved.

I may sound iconoclastic; but the fact is, the idol of evangelism *has* distracted us from the worship of the living God, in more ways than many dedicated leaders and sincere believers realize. It was hard for me to adjust to the proposition that our first sacrifice ought to be the sacrifice of praise; that our first work ought to be the humbling of ourselves in His presence.

When the Bible says that no flesh shall glory in His presence (see I Corinthians 1:29), it would have us understand that our self-generated zeal, however well-intended, is unworthy of credit if God Himself is secondary in our pursuits. Anything we accomplish of lasting significance will not be by the might of our minds nor the power of our plans, but "by My Spirit, saith the Lord of hosts" (Zechariah 4:6, KJV).

It was difficult for me to change my mind. Would I lose my concern for evangelism? Was I drifting toward a dreamy vision of misty-eyed worship for its own sake?

I studied the book of Acts for answers, and marveled at how obvious it was:

1. At Pentecost, when 3,000 souls were saved, the day began with a prayer meeting and proceeded by the Spirit's power into a *worship* service: They all spoke "the wonderful works of God" (Acts 2:11). Supernaturally-inspired worship drew the crowd and created the opportunity for preaching the gospel (verses 1-11).

2. After that, the people were daily at the Temple "praising God" (2:47). Thus, they enjoyed such favor among all the people that souls were being added to the church every day by the working of the Lord Himself (verse 41).

3. The miracle at the Beautiful Gate (Acts 3) happened as Peter and John were on their way to *worship*. The lame man's healing, Peter's sermon and the mighty ingathering of souls were byproducts. They had come to worship God.

There is no more profound example of worship as the key to the early church's discovery of God's methods than the one that occurs in Acts 13. It was "as they ministered unto the Lord, and fasted" (verse 2) that the Church came to a pivotal point in its history. The Holy Spirit summoned Barnabas and Saul (Paul) into missionary evangelism *in the midst of brethren at worship!* Not only did the gospel break through to the entire Roman world, but it actually set the course for the whole westward flow of history.

The very fact that we study Western civilization as a subject in our colleges and universities today is related directly to a worship service among a group of saints in Antioch-on-the-Orontes sometime over 1,900 years ago.

## Ministry to the Saints

The Bible frankly calls imperfect people "saints." Their holiness is secured, not through their own righteousness but through that of Christ Jesus. Then, as partners in this calling, saints are to edify, encourage, care for and love one another as fellow saints.

That's fellowship, and it was hard for me to prioritize this above evangelism in the order of the church's ministry, as the conference suggested it should be. Worship, I reasoned, is for God, but fellowship is only for people—"already saved" people. It seemed selfish.

And furthermore, "fellowship" smacked of church hall dinners with superficial conversation; of people trying to act or sound adequately pious to qualify for acceptance among other Christians.

But this was nothing of what the New Testament intended by the word *koinonia*. The "fellowship" I had dismissed as unnecessary was never intended at all. What was meant by *koinonia* was an ideal that comes within reach when three things take place: (1) clear definition; (2) the right atmosphere; and (3) honest people.

In the New Testament, *fellowship* means "to share in common." The early church shared meals together often (Acts 2:46); faced crises together (Acts 4:23-24); shared their resources to meet one another's practical needs (Acts 4:34; 6:1); and met together often in their homes (5:42).

The epistles are filled with references of "one-to-another" relationships at every point of love, care, concern, prayer, serving, helping or just being patient with. Their lives became locked in and synchronized with one another. Then, impressively, this intimacy, transparency and unselfishness in fellowship—*preceded by regular and praiseful worship*—seemed to attract the rest of society around them:

And all that believed were together, and had all things common; and sold their possessions and goods, and parted them to all men, as every man had need. And they, continuing daily with one accord in the temple, and breaking bread from house to house, did eat their meat with gladness and singleness of heart, praising God, and having favor with all the people. And the Lord added to the church daily such as should be saved.

(Acts 2:44-47, KJV)

Let the church that would evangelize ask itself: "How many people in our world long for genuine evidence that someone simply cares about them?" When the members of the fledgling church expressed sincere concern by sharing one another's needs, onlookers seeing this fellowship of mutually committed people were drawn to them, caught somehow in what one writer calls "the web of love."

Ministry to the saints is nothing more nor less than a completely openhearted and openhanded availability to love, share, help and care for each other. And it stuns the outsider to an awareness that self-giving relationships are possible in this world.

But full-hearted worship and openhearted fellowship do not just happen. They spring from an atmosphere of understanding and trust. This atmosphere can exist only when: (1) we understand God aright; and (2) the leadership of the church manifest a basic transparency. My own ability to communicate these things began before but developed within our years at Van Nuys.

Let's look at both of these requirements in turn.

*Understanding God Aright.* God, I had learned as a youth, is holy and just. Less clear to me was His fatherly graciousness and mercy. It was not as though no one had spoken to me or showed me these truths concerning the Almighty. But I had been blinded somehow by my own idealism, and by my human inclination to accept condemnation as a required (if not holy) emotion, essential to prompt a devoted quest for true holiness.

My years of study in Bible and theology at LIFE Bible College in the 1950s laid foundations in liberating truth upon which life and ministry could be built. I was taught of God's sovereign love and gift in Christ, and the solidarity of the believer's position before the Father through Jesus' justifying work on the cross.

I discovered the deep, securing peace that begets true personal identity, gained when a person learns to identify with Christ. I gained deliverance from the spectre of condemnation, finding in God's Word that my complete acquittal from sin's record and judgment was secured through the cross.

And I learned the confidence that rises when certainty of victory over one's own carnality becomes credible—a genuine potential through the Holy Spirit's resurrection power channeled to the believer now resting in Christ and in His full provision.

These basic points of biblical doctrine anchored me in a high view of God's holiness and justice, in which context the atmosphere for true *koinonia* could be taught to others—a fellowship based in "that which we have seen and heard" (I John 1:3, KJV).

It is crucial that we make a difference between so-called "fellowship" as fostered in some circles and *koinonia* as generated by the Holy Spirit.

There is a kind of "nice, happy feeling" that ends up as nothing more than a sanctified glad-hand-ism. It requires a person only to seek to be "as noble as possible"; and for all we might commend such sincerity, it can never become truly redemptive. Friendly and kind and generous, yes. But confrontive? No. Dynamically comforting? Seldom. Transforming? No.

A relational emphasis abroad today tends to excuse sinning in a "fellowship of understanding," sold off as a transparency between brothers and sisters who accept everyone. All the words are right, but much is lacking. Fellowship needs truth—the *Word* incarnate and spoken in love. Otherwise there is no dynamic to lift people beyond where they are.

True fellowship shares life-giving power as well as tenderhearted understanding. True fellowship is transparent and trusting; and by walking in the light of that fellowship, lives will be cleansed from bondage and disobedience (I John 1:7). True fellowship accepts people where they are, but loves them forward and upward (John 8:ll).

Our fellowship may be indeed an acknowledged union of casualities in the struggles and failures of life—a band of sinners en route to holiness. But true *koinonia* results in progress, growth and victory, as well as patience and understanding with each other when those graces seem slow in coming.

It is delicate territory, treading the line between humanistic and legalistic theology. On the one hand, grace is exaggerated in the name of gentleness or understanding; and on the other hand, biblical injunctions become nails that seal the coffin of those already wounded by a sense of their own failure.

I sensed something of the challenge to make a space between these two ways of half-truth—a place where people could learn to fellowship in a full understanding of God's call to obedience, but with an equal understanding of His mercy, patience, longsuffering and lovingkindness.

I began to learn to trust myself to proclaim His love, with an ever-deepening conviction about His desire toward and His overwhelming commitment to mankind—to me! It began to affect my thinking thoroughly, my teaching and my leading of others. My convictions about God and man provided a biblical and theological base for cultivating a ministry to the saints—a true loving, accepting, forgiving fellowship among the Lord's people. I was braced against humanistic and legalistic traditions, and grounded in a sense of God's majestic, condemnation-shattering provision for us all in the Lord Jesus' death and resurrection.

Now, committed to pastoring a people toward this threefold emphasis of ministry—placing worship and fellowship even before evangelism—I found a combination of dynamic developments taking place.

I found it far easier to lead people in praise and devoted worship of a God they knew to be compassionate. We were living in the pathway to worship according to the Word, which calls forth worship on the basis of God's graciousness. Note such passages as Psalms 29, 96, 136, and II Chronicles 20:21—all of them finding expression in our common exhortation to "praise the Lord in the beauty of holiness, for his mercy endureth forever."

I had always considered humanly attained holiness a prerequisite to worship. Now my mind was cleared to align with God's revelation, that said in effect, "In My sight you *are* beautifully holy. Praise Me for what I see you to be in Christ, and your worship shall be the pathway unto your transformation into the likeness of My Son. And while that's happening, My mercy will last long enough to see you along the way!"

*Transparent Leadership.* With a freer devotion in worship, I began to explore the second requirement for an understanding, trusting atmosphere—that the leadership of the church manifest a basic transparency.

I was already finding that true *koinonia* could thrive in a climate in which genuine love flowed forth from a people gaining a balanced view of God's unending mercy, leading us toward constant obedience. Now this *koinonia* liberated my own self-disclosure in preaching.

Once I believed seriously in God's patience toward me, as a child seeking honestly to grow up in His will, I was emboldened to share with those I led some of my stumblings and failures as I followed Jesus. Episodes from my own life began to become part of the learning process for the congregation. My teaching continued to be rooted firmly in God's Word, but now I could also illustrate its lessons with cases of my own slowness to learn, inability to understand, stupid sinning and impatient presumptions.

As I learned to understand or laugh at myself, the congregation began to discover God's love, too. We could all accept each other because, as the Gaither lyric puts it, "The One who knows me best loves me most."

The people could now share openly about their needs or areas of conflict, because the pastor himself was showing the way. Each person knew it was "safe" to acknowledge his own weakness and need. But the atmosphere of acceptance was balanced with each person's commitment to grow, allowing the sanctifying grace of the Holy Spirit to bring him into Christ's character and likeness.

This order of fellowship is based on more than syrupy platitudes of acceptance or generalized good will. Such a spirit of trust and transparency is born of solid theology. Because the sovereign God has announced our acceptance in Christ, because the Almighty One has disclosed His patience with our slow growth out of weakness into His strength, therefore we can look up and live.

With our heads held high in praise to Him, it makes it all the easier to turn and honestly look into one another's eyes in open fellowship.

In this atmosphere, evangelism unfolded as a natural by-product. As we worshiped, and as we grew to love the Lord and one another more and more, people came into our midst who virtually fell into our hands. They opened their hearts to Jesus Christ because they were captured by the openhearted Spirit present.

Following worship and our sharing together in circles of fellowship and prayer, I taught the Word of God with a different objective than is characteristic of my background. I set out to edify believers, instead of attempting to appeal to the unconverted or to induce guilt in the backslider. Notwithstanding this apparent lack of evangelistic effort, hundreds came to Christ.

In each service and usually just before we dismissed, I began explaining briefly how anyone might begin his life anew in Christ. I invited anyone to do it. This simple, two-minute invitation, without the prefix of a 20 to 30-minute evangelistic message, has resulted in thousands coming to Christ—nearly 20,000 in thirteen years.

By God's grace, this order of soul-saving vitality will continue in our midst—an order *beginning* with worship, *growing* in fellowship and *issuing* in the transformation of lives. This sequence lays the foundation for evangelism.

But building people on that foundation requires one additional point of instruction. It was during my teaching years at the college that the Holy Spirit taught me what I believe to be the foundational concept for *all* ministry. This is the key to releasing people into Phase Three of the outline for the church's ministry as prescribed by the Scriptures: our *ministry to the world.*

# Chapter 6

# PEOPLE OF THE KINGDOM

How can people be led to "minister to the world"? We were regularly seeing people come to Christ, but I realized there was more to that third facet of ministry than simply making decisions.

To be sure, the flow of wholesome life that proceeded naturally from our path of worship and fellowship was resulting in conversions. But more was precipitating these results than met the eye. People were being "taken captive" to Christ, but our penetration into the world with effective ministry was happening for a reason.

One dynamic point of understanding was helping each member of the congregation view himself as a distinct entity, invading his section of society with life and health. It was the byproduct of a teaching I had developed following a breakthrough in my own perception: that the Lord Jesus intends each believer to be an agent of God's Kingdom in the ordinariness of his life.

Let me describe how this discovery took place.

First, in my church background, evangelism occurred generally in one of two places: in public services designed to persuade the lost to decide for Christ, or in pointed conversations between believers and unbelievers, geared for "witnessing to win souls."

In this system, pastors were to preach the gospel and teach others how to witness. For both tasks, proven methods were demonstrated. Preachers were trained to preach evangelistic sermons and give altar calls, and members were trained in planned conversations usable for personal evangelistic encounters.

I want to say that I carry no brief against *any* approach to evangelism, so the preceding two paragraphs are not critical or antagonistic. Still, I personally felt a need to extend the concept of evangelism beyond these limits; for the call to every-member ministry required each person to perceive of himself more naturally as Christ's person, wherever he was and in everything he did.

Since few church members are going to preach a public sermon, I felt that the method of "ministry to the world" had to extend beyond the concept of sermons and altar calls.

Further, my years of experience in training people for personal evangelism had taught me something else: that the promotion of and instruction in planned witnessing encounters will not enflame most believers. These efforts often ignite more guilt and fear than they do fiery zeal.

Earlier in my life, I had considered any reticence about aggressive witnessing to be a reflection of a person's basic unspirituality. I came to see that, while fear may sometimes obstruct a believer's witness, the hindrance was more likely to be ignorance.

When a believer understands clearly the fact and force of the Kingdom life within him, I discovered, he becomes free to minister with confidence on those opportunities the Holy Spirit brings to him in his everyday life.

Teaching the concept of each believer as a Kingdom person began to result in far more ministry than I had ever seen. It exceeded the best I had ever known to generate through the six-week seminars in soulwinning that I had conducted over the years in many churches, even though thousands of people were trained.

It was not that I no longer believed in these methods. Rather, I was seeking a way to nurture every believer in a concept, instead of simply training him in a method. People who embrace an idea—a point of understanding—can apply it to any situation in life, whereas those who know only a plan for conversation are limited to a situation requiring the manipulation of an encounter to make room for their "message."

Furthermore, Jesus did not direct us only to go and tell people how to get saved. His commision was to speak liberty to captive souls; to heal sick bodies; to bind up broken hearts; to visit the afflicted, imprisoned and bedridden; to offer cooling water to thirsty lips; to restore sight to the blind; and to confront and usurp the control of entrenched demon powers.

Without disparaging planned soulwinning conversations, suffice it to say that Kingdom people need more than a set of words to speak; they need to understand *who* they are, *what* the Church is to be, and *how* they can be exactly that. They need to move into each day as common folk, available to the Holy Spirit's direction and enablement.

The key to my being able to begin infusing believers with this sense of extraordinary ministry within reach of ordinary people was my own discovery of the gospel as Jesus taught it.

For several years, it was my joy to teach the course in Synoptic Gospels (Matthew, Mark and Luke) at LIFE Bible College. In that task, I began to be convinced that much of Christ's Church had never been taught the conceptual keystone for its highest rising to ministry. As I see it, this lies in a clear understanding and sensible response to the heartbeat of Jesus' essential theme: *the gospel of the Kingdom of God.*

I have written elsewhere in a more analytical way on this subject; and students aware of the many differences in interpretation among evangelical Christians will realize that much more remains to be said. Nevertheless, a brief study of this concept will explain what has become the touchstone of ministry in our congregation.

To begin, I marveled that I had not seen it more clearly before. The phrase *Kingdom of God* occurs more than 100 times in the Gospels (or its frequent synonym in Matthew, *Kingdom of heaven;* see Matthew 19:23-24 to verify Jesus' interchangeable usage).

It was the heart of Jesus' message. I was amazed, especially since it had never really been defined for me. The Kingdom of God, for me as for most people, was a vague generic term describing anything or everything of spiritual substance.

Consider some common practices contributing to this ignorance:

1. Offerings are received "to help the work of the Kingdom of God." Consequently, most who grow up in church equate the Kingdom of God with the institutional church. They know the funds are used to keep the local operation going.

2. In preaching and evangelism, John 3:3 is commonly quoted: "Except a man be born again, he cannot see the kingdom of God." Thus, the Kingdom of God has come to mean heaven, since most people assume the real issue in this text is one of destination rather than living dynamic.

3. A young person surrenders to God's call on his life and enters a Bible college or seminary to train for leadership in the church. A neighbor describes him as "having given his life for a vocation in the Kingdom of God." Again, Kingdom equals church.

These ideas are not consistent with Scripture. They miss the mark of establishing in the minds of believers what they need to minister effectively to the world. If people are to see themselves as Kingdom people and function accordingly, three things must happen.

First, they must understand what the Kingdom is and discard mistaken notions such as those already described. Second, they must receive the ability Christ gives, so that each member of His Body can function as a representative of His Kingdom. Third, they must see how they can minister the life of Jesus as agents of His Kingdom.

## The Concept of the Kingdom

Let me share in abbreviated form the concept of the Kingdom as I perceive and teach it.

*Kingdom Rule.* The Bible makes two things clear about the rule of God throughout the universe. First, He is almighty; no power transcends His own (Psalm 19:1-6). Second, He delegates His rule of planet earth to man (Genesis 1:26-28).

The heaven, even the heavens, are the Lord's: but the earth hath he given to the children of men.

(Psalm 115:16, KJV)

*Kingdom Lost.* A double disaster occurred when mankind fell from its place of relationship with God and rulership under God. By submitting to Satan's lies, man lost his place with God and forfeited his rule of this earth under God, yielding it into the hands of the adversary.

*Kingdom Usurped.* Since that time, the rule of the planet has been in the grip of Satan, who is called alternately "the god of this world" (II Corinthians 4:4) and "the prince of this world" (John 14:30). We are told specifically that "the whole world lies in the power of the evil one" (I John 5:19, NASV). In the same sense Paul speaks of "this present evil world" (Galatians 1:4).

*Kingdom Ruined.* What God created and called good has not fundamentally changed, but it has come under wicked, rebellious rulership. Evil rules and multiplies its destructiveness upon mankind. Ironically, most of what people blame God for—heartache, disaster, war, strife, bloodshed, broken lives, broken homes, diseased bodies, suffering, and finally death— are *not* indicative of God's action or will, but are the direct result of man's disobedience and Satan's program of ruin and destruction.

*Kingdom Come.* Jesus the Messiah came, the Son of God as both Savior and King. His mission was not only as the second Adam, to rescue man and restore his relationship with the living God; it was also as the Prince of Peace, to reinstate man to his rightful estate as ruler.

Jesus' ministry demonstrates what happens when God's rule reenters the human scene: "Repent, for the Kingdom of God is here with you now." He summoned people to repentance, to return to the Father. He gave evidence of the presence of the Kingdom in many ways. His phenomenal love, grace and forgiveness; His mighty miracles and healings; His powerful dominion over the demonic—all these confirmed that God's rule was reentering this present world.

Whenever people received that rule by acknowledging His Word, the Holy Spirit of God confirmed the word of the gospel of the Kingdom, as He verified the reality of the presence of the King (Acts 2:22; Luke 24:19; John 3:33-35; 5:19).

*Kingdom Victory.* Throughout His ministry, Jesus trained others for ministry. He told them He would die and rise again, and then be taken from them (Matthew 20:18-19; John 14:19-21). But it was not until after His resurrection that the reality of everything gripped His disciples' hearts. They began to understand that His death, resurrection and ascension had conquered hell and broken Satan's death grip on man and planet.

*Kingdom Promise.* Christ promised that the Holy Spirit would make the Kingdom of God work through His disciples, just as it had through Him. Jesus had said:

Truly I say to you, He that believes on me, the works that I do shall he do, and greater works than these shall he do because I go to the Father. And whatsoever you shall ask in my name, that will I do, that the Father may be glorified in the Son. If you should ask anything in my name, I will do it. If you love me, keep my commandments. And I will pray the Father and he shall give you another Comforter, that he may abide with you forever, even the Spirit of truth; whom the world cannot receive, because it does not see Him or know Him: but you know Him, for He dwells with you, and shall be in you.

(John 14:12-17)

He had also taught them, "I will build my Church," adding that "the powers of hell shall not be able to prevail against it, for I will give you the keys of the Kingdom of heaven" (Matthew 16:18-19). After His resurrection and before His ascension, He went further and told them to expect a new dynamic for ministry through the presence and power of the Holy Spirit (Acts 1:4-8; Luke 24:49).

*Kingdom Power.* The advent of the Holy Spirit at Pentecost launched the Church. He anointed every member with the King's anointing, so that His Kingdom could travel in them with ability and power for each situation encountered. The Church was and is comprised of people who have been born of the same Spirit that begat Jesus, and enabled by the same Spirit that enabled Jesus. Born of and baptized with the Spirit, the Church began to "occupy" (do business) until the King would return (Luke 19:13).

The ultimate glory of His Kingdom *enforced* upon earth is still to come, but meanwhile His Body, the Church, is the fullness of His Kingdom *extended* wherever people receive it.

*Kingdom Authority.* The grounds for all Kingdom authority and dominion, and the basis for all Kingdom ministry, is the cross of Jesus Christ. Christ received all power as a result of His conquest of the powers of hell. His blood and His cross vanquished sin and death, and His resurrection has verified His Kingship. Now that He has ascended to the right hand of the Father, "all things [are] under His feet" (Ephesians 1:22, KJV).

> In his Cross he spoiled all principalities and powers, and made an open spectacle of them, triumphing over them in it.
>
> (Colossians 2:15)

> I pray that you may know . . . what is the exceeding greatness of God's power toward us who believe. It is that mightiness which he worked in Christ when he raised him from the dead, and set him at his own right hand in the heavenlies. There he reigns, far above all principality and power and might and dominion and every name, not only in this world, but also in the one to come.
>
> (Ephesians 1:16, 19-21, paraphrase)

*Kingdom Ministry.* Herein is the concept of the Kingdom of God: that the cross has established the grounds for Christ's new rule of power through His Church's ministry to all the world; and that His resurrection has displayed His mastery over the worst that hell can do (Hebrews 2:14-15); and that now, from His throne on high, He extends His Kingdom enterprises through His Body, each member ministering Christ's life by means of the Holy Spirit in them.

*Kingdom People.* Jesus Christ has not left His Church on earth at the mercy of the elements of this world or of the powers of hell. The Church is Jesus Himself—His life, His power, His fullness manifest by His Spirit.

We ought not to think, therefore, that we are on the defensive or that we are called to preserve the status quo. Instead, as we let Jesus' life happen through us, we will enjoy partnership in His ongoing victory. His glory and triumph flow through the people of His Kingdom, through whom He is touching men and circumstances with divine life until He returns.

*Kingdom Warfare.* This releasing of Kingdom triumph does not preclude the experience of warfare. Trial, weariness, temptation, affliction, attack and depression are frequent experiences of the faithful (Acts 14:21-22). True Kingdom teaching is unafraid to acknowledge the fact that, at times, difficulty or even apparent defeat affect the true believer.

The loss of a skirmish or the endurance of conflict, however, is only part of the pathway toward a new dimension of conquest. "And they overcame him [the devil] by the blood of the Lamb, and by the word of their testimony; and they loved not their lives unto the death" (Revelation 12:ll, KJV). Advance and triumph are ours to claim, but never without a struggle, and seldom without temporary casualties or apparent loss.

All the above sections are but an outline of the concept of the Kingdom of God as taught in the Scriptures. When a believer begins to perceive the truth of God's Kingdom, he needs next to be enabled or qualified with power to serve in Jesus' name.

## Entering the Kingdom

When Jesus said, "The Spirit of the Lord is upon me, for He has anointed me to declare the gospel" (Luke 4:18), He was saying that the fullness of the Holy Spirit is essential to minister the fullness of the Kingdom. His own ministry did not begin apart from His baptism in the Jordan and His reception of the Holy Spirit, who descended upon Him after He came up out of the river (Luke 3:21-22).

The sequence of the Holy Spirit's activity in Jesus' life is worthy of review: first He was born as a result of the Holy Spirit's work (Luke 1:35), and later He was empowered by the Holy Spirit for the pursuit of ministry (Luke 4:14).

Similarly, once a believer has been "birthed" by the Spirit into the Kingdom of God, he needs to recognize that Jesus wants each of us to receive the Spirit's power to spread the same good news of life, health and deliverance that He did.

We need to receive the enabling that He promised: "John truly baptized with water, but you shall be baptized with the Holy Spirit . . ." (Acts 1:5).

Sight is the firstfruit of being born into the Kingdom of light. New birth opens our eyes to spiritual things: "Except a man be born again, he cannot *see* the Kingdom of God" (John 3:3, KJV, italics added). But the second need is for might—ability, strength, power—to function as serving sons and daughters of God.

The pathway to power is through water baptism and subsequent Holy Spirit fullness. Although the meaning of being "born of water and the Spirit" (John 3:5) is often disputed, Jesus seems to be showing these means as spiritual instruments assisting us beyond *sight* ("seeing the Kingdom") to *might* ("entering the Kingdom"), being ready to function as a participant.

These verses have nothing to do with seeing or entering heaven. Instead, they describe what we need from God in order to perceive His purpose and participate in the work of His Kingdom. Every member of Christ's Body is called to do that work.

At "The Church On The Way," we urge every believer to seek Christ openheartedly for the baptism with (or infilling of) the Holy Spirit. Some Christians may debate whether our policy is correct, but they cannot deny that wherever people embrace the baptism with the Holy Spirit, according to the scriptural record of Pentecost, the fruit of abounding New Testament church life flourishes.

We will settle for nothing less. We expect everyone in the congregation of "The Church On The Way" to hunger for, seek and receive this infilling. This is not a legalistic demand, but simply a matter of obedience to Jesus' command: "Receive ye the Holy Ghost" (John 20:22, KJV).

Peter's exhortation makes it equally clear that the will of God calls us to receive the same infilling of the Holy Spirit that characterized the church at Pentecost:

Repent, and be baptized every one of you in the name of Jesus Christ for the remission of sins, and you shall receive the gift of the Holy Spirit. For the promise is unto you, and to your children, and to all that are afar off, even as many as the Lord our God shall call.

(Acts 2:38-39)

As to the frequent question of whether today's believer should expect the same evidences of Spirit-filled life reported in the New Testament, we refuse to be argumentative; but the answer is yes. We expect to see the fruit of the Spirit, the love of God, the character of Christ, obedience to the Word and the gifts of the Spirit—all beginning and increasing in the believer as a result of his being filled with the Holy Spirit.

As to "speaking with tongues," we normally experience that grace. We do not pressure a superficial experience, nor do we disapprove of any who have not yet experienced the exercise of spiritual language in their lives. We simply maintain an atmosphere of trust and fearlessness, knowing that the Lord will not make a fool of anyone.

God is seeking a childlikeness in everyone; and there is something about the dependency of the one thirsting after righteousness and the simplicity of submitting to Holy Spirit-enabled utterance that humbles us all as children.

Enough Bible passages relate glossolalia to the occasions when individuals received the Holy Spirit that we know we are not expecting anything unscriptural. (See, for example, Acts 2:1-4; 10:44-46; 19:1-6.) Thus, with faith in God's Word, we encourage people to allow this expression when they ask Jesus to baptize them with the Holy Spirit.

And *He* is the One to ask. As we teach and lead toward being filled with the Spirit, we always focus on Jesus Himself, the Baptizer, rather than on an experience for its own sake. As John the Baptist said:

He that sent me to baptize with water, the same said unto me, Upon whom thou shalt see the Spirit descending, and remaining on him, the same is he which baptizeth with the Holy Ghost.

(John 1:33, KJV)

He will fill all who come to Him, for He said, "Blessed are those who hunger and thirst after righteousness, for they shall be filled" (Matthew 5:6). It was Jesus Himself who also affirmed His Father's willingness in this matter: "If you, being evil, know how to give good gifts unto your children, how much more shall your heavenly Father give the Holy Spirit to them that ask him?" (Luke 11:13). The members of the Godhead combine to make this a beautiful and fulfilling experience for those who, simply and obediently, ask.

We do not, nor will we ever, suggest that to speak in tongues places a person at a higher level of spiritual experience than someone else. It is impossible to gain a higher status than a blood-bought, redeemed, forgiven newborn son or daughter of the most high God.

But the multiple benefits of spiritual language are too valuable to forego. The devotional exercise of "tongues" (not to be confused with the public gift) is extremely practical. It is useful for worship (Acts 2:11), for prayer (I Corinthians 14:2), for intercession (Romans 8:26-27), and for praising ("giving thanks," I Corinthians 14:17).

A person's private devotional life is unquestionably enhanced by a sane, scriptural exercise of spiritual language. This focal point of division among some in the Church has never been divisive among us. Within our Body life, we minister this truth and invite respondents with a naturalness that is neither threatening nor fanatical. And beyond our Body life, we refuse to project a self-righteous or crusading spirit toward churches or believers of a different persuasion. We are more concerned with loving and living in unity than in trying to prove our point.

If our approach is valid, it will verify itself—not in our doctrine but in our devotion to Christ's whole Body, and in our dynamic to serve the world for which He died.

## Ministering the Kingdom

Understanding the concept of the Kingdom and receiving the enabling of the Holy Spirit does not guarantee that a person will minister as Jesus would in a given situation. The people of God are often fat with information and inspiration while remaining slow to integrate truth into action and service. I wish our congregation was always completely and immediately responsive to the truth we receive. We each seem to be growing slowly, requiring more time than we might to assimilate new vision into vital ministry.

But we do minister. And we bear a measure of fruit as we take what we have received and divide it among the needs that we discover readily wherever we go.

If there is any comfort for me in the face of the slowness with which believers respond, I find it in the Word of God. The young church in Acts did not bear fruit by a well-thought-out plan, but by responding to situations they encountered:

Peter's sermon on Pentecost was provoked by the question of onlookers, not by an organized plan developed among the newly Spirit-filled.

The healing of the man at the Beautiful Gate was a response to his request for an alms gift. Peter and John did not get together with an overwrought idea about "ministering healing to that man we've seen sitting there so many years."

The revival in Samaria (chapter 8) happened when Philip was driven there in flight from the persecution of the church in Jerusalem—hardly a carefully planned evangelistic crusade.

This is no case against planning or programs. It is simply a fact that at least as much "just happened," through people who were available to the Holy Spirit, as happened on purpose. Yet we ought not to consider those things that "just happened" as random. They reflect the purposed program by which Christ works in His Church when He finds people who understand and are enabled to work in the Kingdom.

Then, as people of the Kingdom, we need not be pretentious. Few things concern me more about some circles of Spirit-filled believers than their overriding concern to seem very spiritual. It bothers me when people adopt artificial or unnatural behavior in the name of spirituality:

- The organ-like intonation of spiritual terminology;
- The glassy-eyed look of supposed sincerity;
- The Mona Lisa smile of all-knowingness;
- The exclusionary laughter of the "in group";
- The sudden burst of trumpeted "tongues" shattering the beauty of a worship time;
- The need to be known as one who has attained a great status in the Kingdom;
- The sweaty competition of out-testifying the last champion.

The type and tone of supposedly "spiritual" behavior troubles me. And I'm bothered by this for better reasons than mere personal distaste. It disturbs and hurts me because I think people who do these things lack security and the healthy sense of identity and sensibility that Jesus wants for each of us.

Jesus possessed balance. He was the ultimate saint, but He mixed with notorious sinners. He was at times the most sensitive respondent, while at other times He was the boldest initiator. On one occasion He shouted aloud in the Temple courtyard; later He knelt silently at the same location to write with His finger in the dust. There is, in whatever one studies of Jesus, everything of humanity and nothing of superficiality; everything of godliness and nothing of religiosity.

Jesus ministered the joy, life, health and glory of His Kingdom in the most practical, tasteful ways. There is nothing of the flawed habit of hollow holiness or pasted-on piety that characterizes much of the Christianity the world encounters. My plea for a greater degree of naturalness and human sensitivity in ministering Kingdom power and authority is a summons to balance. Bringing the Kingdom of God to people was for Jesus Christ, and is for His Church today, neither a casual nor a passively informal activity. But neither does it need to be flavored by the pushiness, desperation, artificiality or pompousness that bespeaks more an effort born of insecurity or self-righteousness than a ministry flowing naturally from a sensed debt of love.

That last phrase is crucial. II Corinthians 5:9-21 appoints us to minister the reconciling word of God's Kingdom to everyone. The apostle Paul is unabashed in describing his personal motivation for ministry. A powerful inner constraint drives him, because the ultimate issues are eternal: people will be saved or lost, reached or forsaken, and will go to either heaven or hell. There is nothing casual about it.

But neither is there the intensity that some manifest—a zeal that can be counterproductive, since it may cause the proposed recipient of the ministry to become "gunshy" of any contacts with the Kingdom.

Much evangelism, prayer, giving and ministry by sincere believers is motivated by guilt—more than we recognize. Guilt is only another form of fear and is devoid of true love, as are all other kinds of fear.

Inhumanly religious, pious or evangelistically brutal actions leave serious bruises. Can fear minister love? Can guilt minister forgiveness? Can zeal substitute for wisdom? I submit they cannot, and recommend that the ministry of every believer is more likely to surface when he can perceive of himself as an available agent of Jesus rather than as an activist zealot.

We seek at "The Church On The Way" to teach constant availability to the Holy Spirit. This means the believer always conceives of himself as a Kingdom person. He does not have to get some feeling or push a point; he *does* have to be sensitive to the simple promptings of the Holy Spirit.

These promptings will come most likely through the natural social interactions of daily life: prayerful preparation of the heart day-to-day; faithful growth through regular feeding on the Word; warmth of spirit sustained through consistent fellowship with the Body; integrity in relationships so that those around them learn they are reliable people. These are basic ways that Kingdom people operate.

Their witness flows naturally and credibly because they display a blend of sensible humanness and spiritual dynamic. They love, but they do more than that; they serve. Pure, serving love is far more than mere philanthropy. The Spirit of God pervades everything Kingdom people say and do.

They are the new breed of people whom Jesus Christ has rescued from a world dominated by carnality and demonically inspired machinations. He has filled this new race with His life-giving Spirit, taught them with His Word-wisdom, and commissioned them to go, "heal the sick, cleanse the lepers, raise the dead, cast out devils: freely you have received, freely give" (Matthew 10:8). With them we begin to learn to do that, in His all-powerful name and by His all-loving Spirit.

## *The New Breed*

There's a brightness on their countenance,
A power in their hands:
With a sure word of authority they speak.
With the scholar they're conversant,
Understanding with a child;
Apt at warfare—or to turn the other cheek.

For this special breed of person
Has a precious freedom found;
From conformity's ice-prison they have thawed.
And in liberty they function,
Like a troop from worlds unknown.
They have come—the thrice-anointed sons of God.

Purged by water, blood and fire;
By the Word and through the cross,
Then baptized in Pentecostal tongues of flame:
They have struck the crucial balance—
Heed the law and live by grace.
They have learned the conq'ring power of Jesus' name.

So behold, world: your deliv'rers.
And behold, hell: here your fate.
You can recognize them by the glory shown
In their faces—light they captured
In the face of Christ the Lord.
He's their Captain—they His mast'ry gladly own.

Yes, there's brightness on their countenance,
There's power in their hands:
And they valiantly shatter evil's sway;
Tread on scorpions and serpents,
Heal the sick and raise the dead.
They're the radiant legions bringing God's new day.

—J.W.H.

# Chapter 7

# THY KINGDOM COME

*God's purpose in calling us to worship has as its goals encounter and action. He wants to meet with us and move among us, to bring interaction with and transformation of His people.*

This idea is foreign to most churchgoers, who differ in their views on the purpose of worship. For some, worship is meditation and contemplation. For others it is culture and education. For still others it may be inspiration and affirmation—a restatement of one's faith.

As valid as each of these aspects of worship may be, and as proper as they are as a net result of one's having worshiped, none is central to the purpose God proposes in His Word.

In both Old and New Testaments, God's revealed will in calling His people together is that they might experience His presence and power—not as a spectacle or sensation, but in a discovery of His will through encounter and impact. Such times of congregating will beget new capacities and deeper confidence for living and serving.

The Scriptures show this fact and indicate God's desire that people worship Him, for *worship is the means by which a place is prepared for God to meet with and move among His people.*

In directing the building of the Tabernacle, the Lord told Moses to say to the children of Israel:

Let them make me a sanctuary; that I may dwell among them
. . . . And there I will meet with thee, and I will commune with
thee. . . .

(Exodus 25:8, 22, KJV)

In the New Testament, Jesus accents the same thought:

Where two or three are gathered together in my name, there am I
in the midst of them.

(Matthew 18:20, KJV)

The epistles support and advance this idea, as both Paul and
Peter write concerning the Church:

In whom [Christ] you also are builded together for an habitation of
God through the Spirit.

(Ephesians 2:22)

You also, as living stones, are built up a spiritual house, a holy
priesthood, to offer up spiritual sacrifices acceptable unto God by
Jesus Christ.

(I Peter 2:5)

Both of the latter references may refer to the Church more
generally, rather than only to believers' gatherings, but the
words *together* and *spiritual sacrifices* seem to justify applying
them to corporate worship. They are *together,* and the express
purpose in God's mind is that together we become a "habitation" or spiritual house, a place for God to dwell in our midst.

At the risk of laboring a point, I want to say that I am
troubled because, for the most part, believers gathering for
worship generally do not expect God to: (1) be present in a
distinct and profound way; or (2) do anything especially dis-
cernible. Yet the Word of God says plainly that He wants to be
with and work among people in a distinct way when they
gather to worship Him. As Jesus said:

The hour is coming, and is even now already, when true worshipers shall worship the Father in spirit and in truth: for the Father
is seeking such ones to worship Him.

(John 4:23)

This text shows God as on a quest ("seeking") for people
("true worshipers") who will make their times of corporate
worship to be times of spiritual life ("in spirit") and biblical
balance ("in truth").

God is not administering a Bible quiz on Sundays, checking
to see that everyone makes the right kind of doctrinal and
biblical sounds so that He can justly bless them the following
week. Nor is He running a celestial attendance contest, col-
lecting evidence to be presented on Mondays before some
universal tribunal where His credibility may be in question.

We do affirm our faith in God when we worship, and our
presence in assembly may constitute a kind of witness to our
society. But neither of these facts is the primary purpose for
which God has commanded worship.

Nor are our gatherings planned only to reinforce our walk
with Christ. True, both the teaching of Scripture and our
mutual fellowship with one another benefit our growth. But
again, these benefits must be understood in light of a greater
fact: that God Himself wants something from these times
when His people assemble. He wants a place to display His
presence, His love, His power and *Himself.*

Believers are to gather to provide a time and place for the
living Lord to manifest His glory. Accordingly, when the
congregation gathers at "The Church On The Way," we expect
something to happen. We do not assemble for a show or even
for a sermon. We present ourselves in worship purposing to
provide a place for God to make an entrance among us, to
shape us, to work among and through us.

But let me emphasize: my background made it a slow learning process for me to arrive at something of this understanding.

In my upbringing, I had often heard leaders invite worshipers to praise the Lord, citing the text: "The Lord inhabits the praises of His people." Later, as I began my own pastoral ministry, I remember once trying to find that verse in the Bible. Using my concordance, I began with *inhabits* and found nothing. I looked up *people* and drew another blank. Frustrated, I started over; and finally, under *inhabitest*, I found the words that for so long had been misquoted to me and by me:

> But thou art holy, O thou that inhabitest the praises of Israel.
> (Psalm 22:3, KJV)

I pursued a study of the text, discovering that the verb *yawshab* ("inhabit") means, more literally, "to sit down, to dwell, to remain." The Hebrew word works flexibly so as to characterize the person whose action it describes. To describe a judge, for example, it might be translated, "seated in court" or "in judgment"; or of a teacher, "seated in class to instruct."

Thus, in Psalm 22, where the ruling, almighty God is in view, several modern versions appropriately render it, "You are holy, who are *enthroned* upon the praises of Israel." In short, the King of the universe makes His throne to descend in the place where people praise Him.

By the time we came to Van Nuys I was reasonably aware, through this and other Scriptures, that God wants a people who will gather regularly to praise and worship Him, and will welcome His workings in their midst. But a whole skein of lessons were yet to come.

To begin with, I had to learn to expect and contend for the spirit of praise in the services.

At first it did not come readily—not that the small congregation we inherited was resistant. That little group of dear people had an extended history—some as many as 50 years—of worshiping God openly and expressively. But no tradition is a guarantee of dynamic; and in this case, looking back, I believe

most of them would acknowledge that their praise had become perfunctory and programmed.

Sincerity notwithstanding, any people can fall into the trap
of being as those Jesus addressed in the words of Isaiah:

> This people honor me with their lips, but their heart is far from
> me. Howbeit in vain do they worship me . . . .
>
> (Mark 7:6-7; *cf.* Isaiah 29:13)

Furthermore, and quite apart from the people themselves,
the building's sanctuary possessed a strange and oppressive
atmosphere. It wasn't a matter of aesthetics, since the simple
building, modeled after a World War II Army post chapel, was
rustic and rather inviting. Yet one felt a clamminess at times, a
coldness not unlike the quenching effect when a certain person brings gloom or heaviness to a group. "A wet blanket," we
say. It almost seemed as though a personality resided in that
room—someone intent on hindering a free, wholehearted
worship within those walls.

It was not my imagination. Other people mentioned it, too.
Whenever they did I usually passed by their observation,
preferring to avoid anything that could engender either a
negative or superstitious way of thought.

As I became increasingly aware of this clammy presence, a
portion of God's Word came to mind—an unusual passage in
Leviticus (14:33-53) that instructs the people of Israel in the
proper way to cleanse a house contaminated with leprosy.

It seems strange to think of disease infecting a *place*, but it
helped me to take the problem seriously and not dismiss my
heavyhearted feeling as illusory. Consequently, I determined
to do something about it.

Several times each week I made a point of walking through
the sanctuary when no one else was there. Each time I did, I
would lift my voice, shout the praises of God and clap my
hands, declaring the glory and honor of our Lord Jesus Christ.
I rejoiced in the Spirit and with singing, with a sense of

commitment to praise God in defiance of whatever made the place so gloomy spiritually.

Through this kind of spiritual combat, joined to our steadfastness in corporate praise (although I never made public mention of the "clammy presence" issue), we eventually realized a victory over that spirit of heaviness (see Isaiah 61:3).

The crisis in the struggle against that oppressive presence took place, interestingly enough, on Reformation Sunday in October 1970. One of the congregation brought a word of exhortation that we should praise the Lord. It was spoken graciously and perfectly in order, but a bewildering thing happened: no one did or said anything in response. I had expected the people to respond with upraised hands and voices and begin praising the Lord. But nothing happened.

I hardly knew what to do. I was reluctant to speak up because a number of visitors were present. (Sadly, every pastor is tempted from time to time to make the church "look good" to visitors.) Now, if I confronted the congregation's unresponsiveness on the spot, it could disturb the smoothness of the service's flow.

But then and there I decided never again to condition my response to God with a concern about pleasing man.

I came down from the pulpit area, stood in front of the congregation—about 100 were present—and said: "First, I want to say to any who are visiting that I hope you will not be uncomfortable by reason of what I am going to say. Please understand my desire to make you feel welcome, but at the same time I must, as pastor of this flock, speak a few words of rebuke."

Then I changed my tone, not to accuse but to express my pain: "Church, do you realize what we have just done? God, by His Holy Spirit, has just called us in a beautiful and gracious way to praise Him for His great love and goodness to us, and we have responded with silence. I know neither you nor I want to disobey the Word or the Spirit. So we are going to stop everything and give ourselves to worship and praise, until together we sense that we have adequately responded to God's call to worship."

And we did. We stood and sang a song of praise. After that we worshiped, speaking forth the glories of the Lord. And in the next few minutes, the room seemed to brighten—not visibly, but in a way that anyone present could tell we had done the right thing.

That same evening, while the congregation was singing a series of hymns, I turned to Chuck Shoemake, seated beside me on the platform.

"Chuck," I exclaimed, "a tremendous spirit of joy and liberty is here tonight!"

He agreed with a smile, nodding his head and continuing to sing along with the people. I dismissed the matter until it came to mind the following week, another of those times in which the Lord spoke to me.

He spoke on a Tuesday, as I was driving home after lecturing at the college: *The reason for the liberty you experienced Sunday is that the hold of that spirit that has oppressed the church has been broken.*

My spirit leaped within me, and I began to smile to myself. Something wonderful *had* taken place, and my heart was gladdened. The same gladness has continued upon the countenance of this congregation ever since. Something was broken, and praise has flowed freely since that day.

In thy presence is fulness of joy; at thy right hand there are pleasures forevermore.

(Psalm 16:11, KJV)

Today praise begins so spontaneously, and people enter with such joy and liberty into the services at "The Church On The Way," that unless someone was there in that first year-and-a-half, he cannot imagine the struggle we encountered. But since that spirit was broken, our gathering times have become occasions of true joy.

It is not a matter of pumping up praise with superficial pep talks. Instead we simply and warmly encourage everyone to offer loving worship to God. The results are always the same: (1) the presence of God invades the atmosphere; (2) the people truly rejoice in Him; and (3) the Word of God and faith become alive for the duration of the service. The Lord visits us.

It was worth it to keep praising for months in the face of that oppression! And it was worth it to risk the displeasure of a few visitors. Indeed, it was only three months after this incident that the Lord said, "I have given My glory to dwell in this place."

Meanwhile, an intruder had been evicted. The house was being prepared for the abiding presence of Him unto whose praise it had been built.

## Additional Lessons

*Thy Kingdom come, Thy will be done on earth as it is in heaven.*
Familiar words, but what do they mean? Most people, I am convinced, take them as I once did. I thought those words were a prayer for the future—for the "someday" when Christ will come again and exercise His perfect Kingdom on earth.

That day is coming, of course, and we should pray for it. But we ought to pray for it in the words John uses to conclude the canon of Scripture: "Even so, come, Lord Jesus" (Revelation 22:20). Or Paul's *Maranatha!* may spring forth from our lips in anticipation that "the Lord is coming!"

For here is the distinction I had failed to recognize: that Jesus intended *Thy Kingdom come* to be upon our lips not for His future Kingdom, but in intercessory prayer for this present era of the Church's ministry.

Worship is related to the entry of God's rule. The Lord's Prayer teaches it. Opening with praise, the prayer proceeds to call for the entry of God's ruling presence in Kingdom power: "When you pray, say, 'Our Father in heaven, holy is your

Name.' " There is the call to worship, not unlike the "Holy, holy, holy" that pervades all worship around God's throne.

The more familiar word in this part of the Lord's Prayer, in the Old English, is *hallowed*, which has tended to remind us primarily to revere God's name. But Jesus is saying, "When you pray, begin with worship. On the basis of your relationship with the loving Father, proceed to worship Him for His worthiness and glory."

Then Jesus instructs us to pray, "Thy Kingdom come—here as there!" The time is now, and the prayer is definitive: "Let it come at this point in time." The Greek here is active, imperative. (An examination of the whole passage of Matthew 6:9-13 is developed in my book *Invading the Impossible*, a study of effective prayer.)

As we grew in worship, we learned more and more about the presence of the Kingdom, and how God works in the midst of His people, saving, healing, transforming and advancing His purpose in them as they walk in praise-filled worship.

We learned additional lessons during a two-week span in August 1973. Several things happened that greatly enhanced my perspective on the idea that God is enthroned upon the praises of those who worship Him.

Our pastoral staff customarily gathers late on Saturday evenings to pray for the Sunday services. One such night, while we were praying, I felt moved to ask that we each station ourselves at the four corners of the sanctuary and extend our hands as though we were lifting up a canopy.

In fact, a command seemed fixed in my mind—*Lift up a canopy*—and I felt that somehow our praises were providing a tabernacle-like dwelling place for the Lord.

As we did so, we all felt a distinct and pervading sense of God's presence as we worshiped. Time passed quickly—nearly an hour while we rejoiced in this marked sense of God's pleasure with our adoring praise.

Two Saturdays later as we gathered, I again felt prompted to "go and stand at the four corners." I hesitated. I resist doing anything just for its own sake, or as a carnal or humanized attempt to "get a feeling." I don't want to become as a people who think they need always to sit at a certain place, or kneel a certain way, or pray with a specific tone of voice in order to contact God. Such habits soon smack with superstition, and do not characterize the creative and original ways in which the Holy Spirit works.

But I overcame my hesitance. I told the other men, "I don't want to appear as though I'm trying to get something going, or establish a tradition, or anything like that, but I think we're supposed to stand in praise at the four corners again."

We did. The men understood my attitude and joined me as we went to the corners of the room and stood facing the center, joining in prayer and praise as before.

Only a few minutes later Paul Charter said, "Fellows, I don't know how this is going to impress you, but I believe the Lord has just shown me something. Let me submit this to you for judgment, because, even though it may sound strange, I believe it's from the Lord."

We encouraged him and he proceeded.

"The Holy Spirit is showing me that the reason it seems so appropriate for us to stand as we are, at the four corners of the building and worshiping the Lord in this way, is that there are four angelic beings stationed at the same locations. It's as though we are partnering with them in worshiping God."

None of us felt either excited or critical about what Paul had shared. We accepted his words, attaching no particular significance to them, but not knowing of anything in the Scripture against them, either.

We were not worshiping the angels, of course. That would be unscriptural (Colossians 2:18; Revelation 19:10). Rather, if what Paul Charter had expressed were so, we were harmonizing with worship that was already in progress, both in the visible and the invisible realm. It was an insight, but it spoke nothing more to our understanding at the time.

I have often shared what follows in conferences of thousands, and in special seminars with pastors around the world. Although it is always somewhat awkward, since it could be foolishly perverted or misunderstood, I have felt free to minister it. I have learned that my personal presence is sufficient to assure my hearers that I am neither gullible nor goofy. On the other hand, the unique lesson I learned can be at once so humorous and so holy that I am generally not quite certain how to present it. Nonetheless, I proceed.

About ten days after the evening Paul Charter had spoken about angels being at the four corners of the building, I was at the church for a 6 a.m. prayer meeting with some of the men of the congregation.

If revelation depended upon how one feels, I would have been the last candidate in the world that day. I wasn't sick, but having to get up at 5:30 does not begin my day with a thrill. That time of day seems more like "yesterday" to me, and I cannot help suspecting that it does not honestly become "today" until after 6 a.m.!

In any case, while I was kneeling with the others in prayer over various requests inscribed on cards that people had turned in or mailed to us, the Lord spoke to me. What He said baffled me no end:

*The four angels that Paul mentioned the other night are the four living creatures described in Revelation chapter four.*

"Pardon me, God," I felt like saying.

Here I was, trying to pray like a faithful believer, and the God of the heavens (I knew it was He, for I do recognize my Father's voice) was speaking a peculiar thing. I was tempted to say, "Sure, Lord, of course," in the same way one might patronize an excitable child who had just "seen" something.

*Why, entire cult systems have begun with less material than this!* I thought to myself.

But this was no joke; the Lord had said something to me. I stopped, thought a moment, opened the Bible and read that passage of Scripture.

The angelic beings in Revelation 4 are the cherubim. They are mentioned elsewhere in the Word, and are always associated with the throne of God. A thorough study of their appearances in Scripture seems to indicate that they are the worship leaders extending the glory of God throughout all creation. In Revelation 4, for example, at first we see these four beings at worship. But apparently through their summons, the circle of worship continues to expand, so that chapter 5 concludes with a universal multitude joining in.

What caught my attention most, however, was not the angelic beings themselves, so much as their position around the throne.

And before the throne there was a sea of glass like unto crystal: and in the midst of the throne, and round about the throne, were four living creatures . . . .

(Revelation 4:6)

Their being "round about" and four in number *was* reminiscent of the words Paul had shared a few nights before. Still, I really didn't understand anything of abiding substance; and, hesitant to pursue the matter, simply forgot it.

If I had labored for a meaning at any of the three points—the night Paul shared the idea, the morning the Lord gave me Revelation 4, or in the days following that morning—or if I had struggled in any attempt to "make something" of all this, I would frankly doubt my conclusions. But I did not seek an explanation, nor did I even think any further about it.

About two weeks later, however, as I was walking toward the church building from my car, not even asking or thinking about the subject, God showed me the meaning of these words in one simple, clear insight.

I had already satisfied myself that God was *not* saying that the four cherubim who surrounded His throne had now relocated at our address. That was ludicrous. I had also sensed He was teaching me a principle, one applicable anywhere that God's people truly worship Him.

Now, in a micro-second, without any computation or analysis on my part, the Holy Spirit settled the following points of understanding into my soul.

1. Every picture of God's throne shown in the Bible describes both His glory and the presence of these angelic beings (Isaiah 6; Ezekiel 1; Revelation 4).

2. The position of the four angelic beings is *central* to the throne—i.e., in immediate proximity; and *round about* the throne—i.e., at four points in circumference (Revelation 4:6).

3. These creatures lead and stimulate praise, and seem to seek to draw all the earth into chorus with their worship of the Creator (Isaiah 6:3).

4. As a congregation, we had set ourselves to be a people of continued praise and worship, who honor God's Word and glorify God's Son. The Bible says God is enthroned upon those praises (Psalm 22:3).

Then, incredibly, astonishingly and preciously, the Holy Spirit helped me to see a magnificent reality I would never otherwise have grasped: *that the congregation's worship had brought this house of worship into biblical alignment with the throne of God.* The angelic beings had not taken their stations at *our* address; rather, our commitment to worship had aligned us with *God's* address!

I also realized that the entry of God's Kingdom presence is not our attempt to get God to "move." Instead, as Psalm 22:3

puts it, we move toward Him with praises, continually and in a sustained stance of worship, establishing an alignment that in effect places God's throne in the midst of any people who will to be a people of praise. In James' words, if we draw near to Him, He draws near to us (James 4:8).

The realization of such a commitment from a congregation—to walk in a spirit of worship—does not happen overnight. It is one thing for an individual to open his heart to God's dealing and receive an instant response. It is quite another to see the spirit of worship and praise bred in an entire church. The congregation is then responsible to sustain that holy, wholehearted and understanding worship.

The splendor of His working, here or anywhere, is *not* the result of size, renown, growth or any of the things man prizes.

To my own congregation I often say: "Let every member of 'The Church On The Way' take heed to this. The only height of attainment we want to reach is as worshipers who are well-pleasing to the Father. Whatever else He wants us to become will flow naturally from that."

## The Way We Worship

If worship is tempered by a quest for the praise of men, or gauged by taste or preference, we will sacrifice the blessing of His presence in power and lose His work of glory among us.

New Testament believers recognized that worship is neither a cerebral pursuit, a heightening of mystical consciousness nor an emotional binge. Worship is man's total being aglow in the life the Holy Spirit imparts, offering spiritual sacrifices:

I beseech you, brothers, present your bodies [physical worship] a living sacrifice [emotional worship], holy and acceptable unto God, which is your spiritual and *intelligent* [Gk.] worship. And be not conformed to this world [which devalues the worship of God], but be transformed by the renewing of your mind [thinking on God's terms, not your own], that you may prove [i.e., discover] what is the good and well pleasing will of God.

(Romans 12:1-2; cf. Hebrews 13:15;<br>I Peter 2:5; Psalm 51:17)

The Greek word for worship—proskuneo—actually means "to prostrate oneself before God." The essence of worship is not a physical prostration in worship so much as the prostrating of our pride before Him. Physical prostration in worship is more suitable for private devotion because of the lack of space in our public worship. But we must lay low our human wills before Him repeatedly, because they rise so readily to contend for their own dignity.

May the Holy Spirit deliver us from vain ignorance, and teach us that our highest dignity is in the sheer nobility afforded us as we enter into the presence of the King with worship, praise and thanksgiving, thereby giving place for His glory to dwell in our midst.

Here is an outline for worship* that we have found helpful:

Let us then worship . . .

1.  . . . with *our regenerated spirit* (Romans 1:9)
    a. Worshiping in spirit (John 4:23-24)
    b. Singing spiritual songs (Col. 3:16; Eph. 5:19)
    c. Giving thanks "well" by the Spirit (I Cor. 14:15-17)

2.  . . . with *our renewed mind* (Phil. 2:3-5)
    a. Worship with intelligent obedience (Rom. 12:1, II Cor. 10:5)

---

* From "The Way We Worship," a series of six messages brought to the congregation of the First Foursquare Church of Van Nuys, Calif., by Pastor Hayford. The tapes of those messages are available through SoundWord Tape Ministry, 14300 Sherman Way, Van Nuys, CA 91405. (Pastors and church musicians may write for information on tapes of leadership seminars on worship and for musical resources for teaching and leading worship.)

    b. Praying with the understanding (I Cor. 14:15)
    c. Praising with the understanding (Psalm 47:6-7)

3. . . . with *our revived emotions* (Col. 3:23; Rom. 12:11-15)
    a. Shouting and clapping hands unto the Lord (Psalm 47:1)
    b. Praising Him aloud with the congregation (Psalm 47:1)
    c. Rejoicing and expressing thanksgiving (Psalm 100:1, 4; Phil. 4:4)
    d. Being silent before the Lord (Psalm 46:10; Hab. 2:20)

4. . . . with *our rededicated body* (I Cor. 6:19-20)
    a. Kneeling in worship (Phil. 2:9-10)
    b. Bowing heads (Micah 6:6-8)
    c. Raising heads (Psalm 3:3-4; Heb. 4:16)
    d. Lifting hands (Lam. 3:40-41; Psalm 63:3-4)
    e. Waving hands in praise (Lev. 9:21)
    f. Dancing with joy before the Lord (Psalm 149:3; 150:4; 30:11)

The above categories and references are only introductory; but as I lead the people in examining and exercising these and other significant biblical guidelines to worship, we experience the benefits of obedience. The issue is God's glory, and the outflow is His Kingdom, here and now!

# Chapter 8

# WHEN WE COME TOGETHER

The flow of the church service is a significant factor in determining the release of a congregation's life and the individual's ministry. These gatherings can be fruitful or frustrating, and the difference is found in the *order*—the sequence, design and direction—of the meeting.

The Bible furnishes an excellent case study of order being retrieved from chaos in one congregation's "services." Since it is doubtful that many have problems of congregational hyperactivity, we can study such a case profitably, for here is apostolic order, in both 1) making room for vital ministry and participation by the membership gathered in assembly; and 2) maintaining a respectful and sensible order in the tenor of their times together.

We will understand I Corinthians 14 best when we recognize that it speaks to a spiritually alive congregation that needed to know how its gathering times ought to be conducted. The various problems debated so often in this text are readily resolved when we see that this young group of Spirit-filled believers was relatively new at worshiping and fellowshiping together.

Their careless spontaneity in expressing spiritual language; their failure to recognize priorities among spiritual gifts; their insensitivity to newcomers in their midst; their apparent inclination to gullibility where prophetic utterance was concerned; their problem with what seems to be an inappropriate takeover of leadership by women—all these difficulties were related to their "church services," as we would call them.

After considerable instruction to help them sort out the difference between private and devotional exercise of "tongues" from the public and prophetic exercise of spiritual language, Paul now inquires, "How is it then, brethren?"

Then he answers his own question by urging *multiple ministries*, but restricting all ministry to only that which edifies: "When you come together, every one of you has a psalm, has a doctrine, has a tongue, has a revelation, has an interpretation. Let all things be done unto edifying" (I Corinthians 14:26).

This statement sets forth two principles:

1. Different members of the assembly will have various things to bring;

2. Everything that is brought should upbuild the assembled body.

To this day, merging these principles is a challenging proposition. Even in a small congregation of 30 or 40 believers, it is difficult to know how everyone can become involved in a positive, contributing way, sharing and edifying the others gathered with them without protracting the service impractically.

Further, the record is well-established that allowing everyone to express himself under the guise of "letting the Holy Spirit have His way" is seldom as edifying as it is time consuming. Thus, most church leaders plan services that may be more efficient, but not very often effective.

Even when the goal of worship and teaching is reached, the pastor must ask the question, "Has each believer's own ministry been expanded, or has only his understanding been enlarged?"

At "The Church On The Way," our gatherings must minister

to the Lord, the saints and the world. Our worship through singing, praise and receiving the Word as it is taught provides the first. Coupled with it, fellowship before and after the service helps to accomplish the second. But the believer must be involved more personally than these activities permit if he is to be more and more ready to fulfill his stewardship of the gospel of the Kingdom.

Fellowship requires direct interaction, not just a few words of conversation preceding and following the service. People cannot grow in learning to minister without more than a set of biblical ideas. They must be introduced firsthand to some pattern of possible responses to the kinds of need they encounter daily.

It is impractical to say, in effect, "Listen to truth here and now, and act on it there and then." It is far better to say, "As you are hearing truth, tell it here; get started in doing the Word in some way *now*." Thus, every gathering should have some opportunity to integrate the truth being taught; to apply it to flesh-and-blood circumstances.

We cannot cultivate every member into daily ministry by reserving training and exercise for annual seminars, weekend retreats or other special series. Instead, almost every time we meet, we must be about mobilizing the membership. This is not a crusade, simply a constant pattern of development, using the most common instrument available to any group of believers—their regular church services.

The words of our Corinthians text calls us to learn "member ministry" while gathered as a congregation. We have sought to answer this call to:

1. Become a congregation that gives place to the gifts of the Holy Spirit listed in I Corinthians 12:8-10 and elaborated on in chapters 13 and 14.

2. Become a congregation committed to the systematic and edifying teaching of the Word of God as suggested in I Corinthians 14:19-20.

3. Become a congregation devoted to the exercise of Holy Spirit-inspired worship, commended in I Corinthians 14:2, 14-17.

4. Become a congregation in which every member is involved as much as possible, as recommended in I Corinthians 14:26.

Now, how can we arrange an orderly service with worship, personal participation, strong Bible teaching and expression of the gifts of the Spirit, all in less than two hours? Before I try to describe how we conduct services at "The Church On The Way," let me establish the three controlling propositions that guide us:

1. We attempt to conduct our gathering times on the basis of what we find in God's Word. We are not trying merely to justify what we want to do.

2. We have distinct goals for each of the three services that comprise the week, and we employ a specific pattern for each one. We also expect the Holy Spirit to work a fundamental creativity within each pattern, and we are more than willing to allow the Spirit to change that pattern at any time.

3. We understand that people may feel uncomfortable in a service that requires forthright participation. However, we gently but firmly refuse to concede to their discomfort. We are willing to lose potential members to a less demanding parish if they are unwilling to be open to their own growth potential. That may sound heartless, but to my mind it is actually a commentary on an unfortunate fact—that growth is not the consistent expectation of congregational life. Mere attendance is too often allowed to substitute for discipleship. (This is not to say, of course, that there are not

positive reasons a person may relocate to another congregation.)

## *What the Bible Says*

Paul wrote I Corinthians 14 to believers who were excessively exuberant and disorderly when they gathered. An equal and opposite error befalls others today who prefer to be spectators. At least the Corinthians were in no danger of that! They needed balance and wisdom; and apostolic instruction and correction was given patiently. By the Holy Spirit's inspiration, that teaching still serves us today.

The next few pages contain a paraphrastic analysis of the text, according to my understanding of it. Please examine it thoughtfully, comparing it with the classical English rendition (or your own more recent translation). Having carefully studied it for years in the light of both the Greek text and the chemistry of vital experience, I believe it provides a Scripture basis for the discreet conduct of lively church gatherings on New Testament terms.

| King James Version: I Corinthians 14 | A Functional Paraphrastic Analysis |
|---|---|
| 1. Follow after charity, and desire spiritual gifts, but rather than ye may prophesy. | *Verse 1:* Love is always paramount and spiritual gifts are desirable, but clear communication is essential when you gather. |
| 2. For he that speaketh in an unknown tongue speaketh not unto men, but unto God: for no man understandeth him; howbeit in the spirit he speaketh mysteries. 3. But he that prophesieth speaketh unto men to edification, and exhortation, and comfort. | *Verses 2–25:* Speaking with tongues in public without interpretation is counterproductive.  The chief benefits of *prayer* with tongues are: communi- |

4. He that speaketh in an unknown tongue edifieth himself; but he that prophesieth edifieth the church.

5. I would that ye all spake with tongues, but rather that ye prophesied: for greater is he that prophesieth than he that speaketh with tongues, except he interpret, that the church may receive edifying.

6. Now, brethren, if I come unto you speaking with tongues, what shall I profit you, except I shall speak to you either by revelation, or by knowledge, or by prophesying, or by doctrine?

7. And even things without life giving sound, whether pipe or harp, except they give a distinction in the sounds, how shall it be known what is piped or harped?

8. For if the trumpet give an uncertain sound, who shall prepare himself to the battle?

9. So likewise ye, except ye utter by the tongue words easy to be understood, how shall it be known what is spoken? for ye shall speak into the air.

10. There are, it may be, so many kinds of voices in the world, and none of them is without signification.

11. Therefore if I know not the meaning of the voice, I shall be unto him that speaketh a barbarian, and he that speaketh shall be a barbarian unto me.

12. Even so ye, forasmuch as ye are zealous of spiritual gifts, seek that ye may excell to the edifying of the church.

13. Wherefore let him that speaketh in an unknown tongue pray that he may interpret.

14. For if I pray in an unknown tongue, my spirit prayeth, but my understanding is unfruitful.

15. What is it then? I will pray with the spirit, and I will pray with the understanding also: I will sing with the spirit, and I will sing with the understanding also.

16. Else, when thou shalt bless with the spirit, how shall he that occupieth the

cation with God (v. 2); the edifying of your inner man (v. 4; *cf.* with Jude 20 and Ephesians 3:16-17); and prayer and worship beyond your intellectual resources (vv. 14–15, 17).

The indiscriminate exercise of tongues in public gatherings defeats your purpose in coming together (vv. 6–8). The purpose is for the *whole* church to be built up and edified (v. 5), which requires those present to understand and participate. This cannot take place as it should (v. 9, 11, 16) unless the congregation adheres to basic order (vv. 12–13).

When you observe proper order in a childlike and mature spirit (v. 20), people will not think you insane (v. 23); but instead, many will be moved and won by the power of the Holy Spirit working in each of you (vv. 24–25).

I am not demeaning glossolalia (v. 18), but am setting an absolute priority and control upon the method of your communications when you assemble (v. 19).

room of the unlearned say Amen at thy giving of thanks, seeing he understandeth not what thou sayest?

17. For thou verily givest thanks well, but the other is not edified.

18. I thank my God, I speak with tongues more than ye all:

19. Yet in the church I had rather speak five words with my understanding, that by my voice I might teach others also, than ten thousand words in an unknown tongue.

20. Brethren, be not children in understanding: howbeit in malice be ye children, but in understanding be men.

21. In the law it is written, With men of other tongues and other lips will I speak unto this people; and yet for all that will they not hear me, saith the Lord.

22. Wherefore tongues are for a sign, not to them that believe, but to them that believe not: but prophesying serveth not for them that believe not, but for them which believe.

23. If therefore the whole church be come together into one place, and all speak with tongues, and there come in those that are unlearned, or unbelievers, will they not say that ye are mad?

26. How is it then, brethren? when ye come together, every one of you hath a psalm, hath a doctrine, hath a tongue, hath a revelation, hath an interpretation. Let all things be done unto edifying.

27. If any man speak in an *unknown* tongue, *let it be* by two, or at the most *by* three, and *that* by course; and let one interpret.

28. But if there be no interpreter, let him keep silence in the church; and let him speak to himself, and to God.

29. Let the prophets speak two or three, and let the other judge.

30. If *any thing* be revealed to another that sitteth by, let the first hold his peace.

31. For ye may all prophesy one by one,

*Verses 26–40:* First, each of you come with something to share, but it *must* be worthwhile (v. 26–31). If you exercise the gift of tongues (*always* with interpretation) or the gift of prophecy, there should be a distinct limitation on the number of participants (v. 27, 29). Those who are mature should be responsible to evaluate what is said (v. 29). This is no restraint upon the Holy

that all may learn, and all may be comforted.

32. And the spirits of the prophets are subject to the prophets.

33. For God is not *the author* of confusion, but of peace, as in all churches of the saints.

34. Let your women keep silence in the churches: for it is not permitted unto them to speak; but *they are commanded* to be under obedience, as also saith the law.

35. And if they will learn any thing, let them ask their husbands at home: for it is a shame for women to speak in the church.

36. What! came the word of God out from you? or came it unto you only?

37. If any man think himself to be a prophet, or spiritual, let him acknowledge that the things that I write unto you are the commandments of the Lord.

38. But if any man be ignorant, let him be ignorant.

39. Wherefore, brethren, covet to prophesy, and forbid not to speak with tongues.

40. Let all things be done decently and in order.

Spirit, but does require Spirit-filled people to restrain themselves (v. 28, 30, 32). God is consistently a God of an orderliness which brings peace when your congregation assembles (v. 33). In this regard, remember three things:

*First*, women are not to be allowed to converse indiscriminately during the gathering time: it can wait until they are home (v. 34, 35—Note: 11:5 makes it clear that women can and do participate. The issue here is appropriate talk and noncontributive comment). *Second*, truly sensible and spiritual members will affirm the wisdom of what I am saying. If they don't, that is their problem (v. 36–38). *Third*, desire clear communication at all times, but that is no argument against the proper place of speaking with tongues (v. 39). Be certain that everything is done in a graciously compelling and decorous manner (Gk. *euschemonos),* and that a sensible sequence and timing is maintained (v. 40).

As cursory as this coverage may be, more detailed examination of the text will bear the weight of the proposition that the

Bible calls for orderly services which release worship, release the flow of gifts, and develop the ministry-mindedness of the individuals present. We conduct our services on these terms.

## The Thrust of Services

*Sunday Morning.* On Sunday morning we gather to carry out the three-fold ministry which characterizes our mission as a congregation. We exalt the Name of Jesus Christ and summon every person to "enter into His gates with thanksgiving and into His courts with praise" (Psalm 100:4). From the platform, we direct prayer, praise and other expressions of worship, but at the same time we try to give simple guidelines to encourage each person to express his own sensitive and thoughtful worship.

Beside meaning-filled choruses, we sing at least one historic hymn to anchor ourselves to the truth which echoes back to the traditional testimony of the people of God throughout the centuries. Although this use of hymnody occupies less than five minutes, we believe this habit to be very significant. By it we declare our commitment to sound doctrine, our respect for the past and our adherence to timeless truths as expressed in the Church.

Ministrytime is usually framed by a focus on the Word of God. We do not interact and pray together merely to exercise humanistic goodwill. Much more than that, we are setting ourselves to apply some truth from the Scriptures. To give depth and biblical purpose to our interaction, I usually explain a text and suggest how to apply it as we minister to one another. Convincing everyone to form small circles of prayer and share is crucial, especially where the visitor is concerned. We do this graciously, but make it clear we are committed to "every member—every person—participating"; and we seek to implement the practice helpfully.

We use songs to emphasize each truth involved in the flow of the service. Music helps sustain a unified focus on the truth being emphasized. We reject the arbitrary selection of choruses as being fundamentally dishonest with God and the congregation. What we speak and what we sing must constantly move toward the goal of the gathering. This direction is at the heart of *order* in a service.

Many people mistakenly consider themselves led of the Holy Spirit, even though the "leading" may cause a service to drift from theme to theme with no coherence. This is not motivated by the Holy Spirit, but by human subjectivity, and is the cause for many pointless gatherings.

Whenever we assemble, everything we do is corporate. We are not conducting private or small group devotions.

Sunday morning is always Easter in a certain respect: it is a renewed celebration of the Lord's Day, the beginning of the new creation in Jesus Christ. It is an affair of state in the Kingdom of God; and, while this does not mean that we bind burdens of exactitude, pompousness or ceremony upon ourselves, it does mean we avoid whatever wastes time or is merely habitual.

Teaching the Word has a large place in this service. We often distribute prepared outlines, designed for both immediate use and later study. We seek to both *mend* and *equip* believers for ministry. People who are tempted, wounded, broken and distressed need to hear the Word. People eager to relate truth to life, and life to those around them, need to hear it, too.

The message of the morning completes the cycle of the threefold ministry:

1. Worship and song, prayer and praise—ministry to the Lord.
2. Prayer and sharing, personal interaction—ministry to the saints.
3. Teaching the truth, preparing for service—ministry to the world.

All of these interrelate, of course, and no dissection is

possible without ruining the whole; but the basic concepts are served in each Sunday morning service.

*Sunday Evening.* While we find a consistent pattern in the Sunday morning service, the evening gathering varies widely in its thrust and application. The common denominator is its focus on our warmth and growth as a family—one body enjoying life in Jesus.

Expositional series elucidate crucial biblical themes for the thinking person in our culture. Musical programs celebrate biblical truths or holidays. Guests or staff speakers address an aspect of life deemed important at the moment.

One or another of things like these constitute the larger part of a given Sunday evening meeting. An opening time of worship is followed by water baptism; and, aside from the principal presentation as mentioned in the above examples, little else is planned.

In every service, however, at any time in the week, what is planned never preempts what may be sensed. A song may ignite an especially remarkable response, and we will give place to the flow of that work of God's grace. We may invite testimonies or a report of some recent event in which God's power was at work. Someone in the congregation may prophesy or exhort us.

But to give a place to spontaneous expression does not require that we give *the* place to it. Because something is allowed, in other words, does not mean that "anything goes." Nor do a few minutes of alteration in the plan mean that the whole plan is scrapped. Beautiful innovations and divine interruptions are welcome. But because we leaders approach our gatherings with considerable prayer and preparation, it generally follows that we have the mind of the Lord for the basic direction of that service.

I hasten to add, however, that we refuse to believe we ever have *all* of that direction in advance. We expect the Holy Spirit to do something lovely and distinctive in each service.

## *Manifestation of the Gifts*

In this regard, it is important to describe how we expect the gifts of the Holy Spirit to function in the public services. We expect gifts to flow through all members of the body (I Corinthians 12); and we maintain order (I Corinthians 14). Taking these as axiomatic, how do we proceed?

Two guidelines serve our congregation well in this regard.

First, since "the spirit of the prophet is subject to the prophet" (I Corinthians 14:32), we do not believe a gift must of necessity "burst forth" uncontrollably. The individual who feels that the Holy Spirit has prompted him or her to prophesy, speak in a tongue, interpret or exercise some other gift is expected to indicate this to one of those leading the service.

There are several times and ways to do this. During worship times, greeting times, ministry times or prayer times, the individual may go to one of the pastors or elders and say what he thinks God is giving him at the moment. Alternatively, an individual could lift his hand and, when recognized, say what he is receiving that he believes to be for the assembly.

Then—and this is the second guideline—it is up to those leading the service to decide what to do. They are not compelled to admit the proposed gift then and there, or even at all. If it does not seem the timing is right, they may ask the individual to wait, or even to share it at another service.

At times sincere people have beautiful insights that are so "electric" to their own soul, since God is dealing with *them,* that they are sure they should share it. Consequently, we often ask people to share what they feel with an elder before they do so with the congregation. The elder may recognize it as a personal insight that is either unnecessary or inappropriate for the congregation at that time.

We risk hurting people's feelings by doing it this way, though I believe we seldom do, but it seems the path of balance between two entirely undesirable courses: (1) giving no place to the Spirit's working; or (2) exercising no control whatever. Both would be offensive to God.

Fears of quenching the Spirit have proven unjustified, and we experience the ongoing ministry of the Holy Spirit to our congregation through words of prophecy, exhortation, wisdom and knowledge.

The third service of the week is the midweek prayer gathering. It is so powerful, joyous and bouyant that it deserves a chapter of its own. God has taught us some of our weightiest and mightiest lessons on Wednesday nights.

# Chapter 9

# THE SPIRIT OF INTERCESSION

Wednesday nights at "The Church On The Way" excite me as much as anything in this world. For most people, the words *prayer meeting* conjure images of a small, musty group of irrelevant people who gather out of superstition, mumble heavenward, and then dissolve quietly into the night. The words carry all the dark and Gothic flavor of *Wuthering Heights*.

Not so here! At midweek service, the church rises in triumph to do its principal work in God's Kingdom. We move into blessed fellowship and powerful unity through worship, and then come to the primary purpose of our gathering: intercession and spiritual warfare. If Sunday morning is an affair of state in the Kingdom, then prayer meeting is congress in session or an army on the march.

## *The Church at Prayer*

The concept of "church" was well-established before the time of Christ. The Greek word translated church is *ekklesia*. It was important to the vocabulary of ancient Greece when the great city-states were being founded.

Primitive government in Greece was essentially democratic. All the people met to decide the issues that concerned them.

When they met together to deliberate, they were the *ekklesia*, the assembly. Whatever the issue—what tax should be levied, what law should apply, what war should be waged—the *ekklesia* exercised the rule.

The *ekklesia* was the net result of calling the proper citizens together. As they took action, so it would be determined and accomplished.

This idea is fundamental to our concept of the people of God at prayer. We base our concept on biblical premises, however, not upon Greek history. Thus, our thinking goes like this: the Holy Spirit exercises the authority of Jesus Christ the Lord through the redeemed citizens of the Kingdom of God. These citizens have been given the keys of the Kingdom—the right to exercise His rule in His name. Jesus said that if they would function in agreement and in the resources He has given them, "the gates of hell [the powers, the government of dark rulers—see Ephesians 6:10-18] shall not prevail against [My church]" (Matthew 16:18-19, KJV).

What Christ accomplished unconditionally in the invisible realm through the cross awaits the application and advancement of the living Church now, conditionally, in the visible realm. This condition is met by proclaiming the gospel, but *all* proclamation and extension of the gospel of the Kingdom is predicated on prayer.

This explains the force and priority of Jesus' words when He declared His intent to build His Church:

| Matthew 16:19 | Conceptual Paraphrase |
|---|---|
| Whatever you bind on earth | Whatever you may at any given point in time *bind* (establish contract concerning or stave off from satanic advance on earth) |
| shall be bound in heaven. | has already been accomplished authoritatively in the spiritual realm of real contest. |

| | |
|---|---|
| *Whatever you loose on earth* | And further, whatever you may at any given point in time release, unlock or forgive concerning any situation or person on earth |
| *shall be loosed in heaven.* | I have already secured the authority for that action in the realm of spiritual struggle through the cross and my resurrection. |

This amplification and paraphrase is entirely justified on the basis of the moods and tenses of the Greek verbs used in this classic passage. Jesus expressed His commitment to build His Church, and thereupon unfolded His plan to endue that people (Church) with power, so that hell should have to yield and give way wherever the Church applied that power.

This is no cheap or easy idea to embrace. Sadly, the phrase the *authority of the believer* has become a slogan, a catchall for easy believe-ism in segments of the Pentecostal and charismatic communities. The words *What you say is what you get* are true enough that they cannot be rejected out-of-hand. I agree that the Bible urges us to utter continually discreet and faith-filled speech. Indeed, personal salvation even begins with it (Romans 10:9-10). And faith does indeed express itself through lips of clay.

In addition, these same lips of clay can dissolve the force and dynamism of some of God's greatest provisions through unbelieving, spiritually scrambled speech. Negativism and doublemindedness must be conquered not only in the heart but on the lips.

The problem with ideas about "faith" as I see it emphasized in some quarters, however, is that many hearers too often translate these truths into using faith to "get the things I want." Also, some well-meaning proponents of this emphasis have cultivated a very real form of selfishness and self-righteousness.

Among devotees in this self-defined circle of "believers," the test of faith becomes one's ability to demonstrate a "product" (healing, money, a new car) with little concern for maturity or character. Testimonies seem to center on "what I got," and seldom place much value on "how I grew," "what I learned through trial," or "how I overcome smallness of heart or mind."

Thus, our own corporate action in spiritual warfare and authoritative prayer is not based on shallow promises or parroted slogans. We have accepted God's summons to bold belief on biblical terms that build character. Our prayer meeting has become a continual, mighty, week-after-week act of faith. We build on the foundation of the cross and commit ourselves to ceaseless intercession, and obey the discipline of fasting according to scriptural guidelines.

Fasting is an instrument of spiritual conflict, and its force invigorates our sustained prayer together as we lay claim to Calvary's victory with direct application to people and nations. We do not always expect easy answers or quick victories, and we refuse to be intimidated or squelched in our zeal by apparent losses, setbacks or stalemates.

The congregation seizes grand issues in prayer—the government of nations, righteousness in lawmaking, the extension of the gospel through barricades of adversity. But that does not keep us from more "homey" issues. We pray for a brother or sister who needs a job; a junior high schooler facing an examination; a man who needs healing from a heart condition; a loved one entering surgery next Monday; a drunken neighbor who has left his wife and kids; a motorcycle accident victim facing amputation; a family that has split up; a woman diagnosed with cancer.

Long-range universal and cosmopolitan issues interweave with immediate personal problems and human dilemma. They are one and the same. We approach both on the basis of our right to invade these issues in prayer, expecting that God's will shall be done in the *here and now,* on earth, as it has already been established *there and then*, in the spiritual realm of the heavenlies through the cross and the resurrection!

Such is the tenor of this midweek meeting. But to understand how this has come about, one must travel through the years of growth, experience, trial and slow learning. The spirit of intercession, a dynamic prayer meeting, and our sense of divine destiny did not arrive overnight; nor will they continue unless we regularly renew our faith, commitment and spiritual stamina.

I want to describe how it all happened under three headings: First, how in the beginning we had to confront a decadent habit; second, how the Holy Spirit called and constrained the congregation, and inaugurated our intercession; and third, how the pattern of our weekly prayer service has emerged from these learning processes.

## *The Beginnings*

Few things are more depressing than a dead prayer meeting! A church's power base, shorn of its life, becomes the Church's most monstrous tradition.

When I came to Van Nuys, I looked at the monster and my heart sank. Could I slay this dragon? Or would it slay me? Resolve settled in my heart. I knew not whence it came, or how; but I would not tolerate defeat. I set about to see that the prayer meeting became exactly that—a *prayer* meeting.

Other congregations have opted for such things as midweek Bible studies, family nights or "total church action" nights, featuring everything from prayer to choir practice. I wouldn't argue against any of these, but I was convinced that the Holy Spirit was calling us to become a people of prayer. Our Wednesday prayer meeting would be our laboratory to research the Church's power potential.

So I announced to my little flock that we were going to pray specifically, in faith, and that we were not going to get bogged down in guessing games about requests and answers.

One Wednesday evening, within weeks of my arrival, someone suggested we "pray for the earthquake in Central America." One of the Latin American republics had been devastated, and it was unquestionably a worthy request.

It was the kind of request, however, that so often people pray over vaguely—so vaguely that no particular answer is sought or noticed. This vagueness derives from a sense of helplessness and compassion mixed with guilt and fear—guilt that others suffer while we don't, and fear over "what if that had happened *here?*" We seldom recognize the guilt or fear; and, to be sure, sometimes they do not exist. But the vagueness remains.

Though this sort of request sounds thoughtful, therefore, it is really a vicious kind of thoughtlessness. It seeks to utilize prayer as an escape from the responsibility to exercise faith or take action. And if prayer can be used so ignorantly in an apparently sincere way, no force remains to sustain the Church's life, because prayer is the breath of the Church.

"That's good," I said to the person who had suggested we pray concerning the earthquake. "That disaster deserves prayer, and the Word of God holds real promise if we pray. How shall we pray about the earthquake?"

At first everyone looked dumbfounded. Such matters, we had all believed (including myself), were simply "put into the hands of the Lord." We supposed that, once we had prayed, God was responsible for whatever might happen.

"I don't want to be difficult," I continued, "but I think we should decide exactly how we are going to pray. It's too easy to speak a few words and let the matter trouble us no more because we have resigned the matter to God. I believe the Lord wants us to learn something through this request.

"First of all, did God will the earthquake? Perhaps—we don't know. But we do know this broken-crusted earth, which trembles as much as it does, is no longer quite the same as the Eden God created. Paul tells us in Romans 8 that man's fall subjected creation to things outside its intended order. I propose that God does not want earthquakes, and probably did not will this one. At the same time, we can probably agree it hasn't surprised Him, either.

"Let's ask the Holy Spirit to show us how we ought to pray about the tragedies of this natural disaster."

Everyone agreed and we asked the Holy Spirit to do exactly that. Then we began to interact over the next few minutes, and we arrived at these requests:

1. Pray for the bereaved, that the Spirit of God would comfort them.
2. Pray against bitterness finding an entrenched place in hearts that would blame God for the earthquake.
3. Pray for gospel workers and believers to demonstrate the love, power and life of Jesus unto the salvation of souls.
4. Pray for rescue workers and relief agencies, that their efforts would be enabled by God's blessing and international help.
5. Pray that our interest would not wane following this prayer time, but that we would continue to pray, and that God would show us how to help in addition to praying.

Can you imagine what happened? The people prayed fervently, with faith and conviction. They sought God earnestly to take a hand in the situation and demonstrate His power. Later they watched the papers and other media for evidence of answers. At the same time, we decided to receive an offering to send to an appropriate relief agency; and, as it turned out, our own denomination became engrossed immediately in such relief through our work there.

Two or three years later, our missionary from that nation visited our congregation and told us what happened following the earthquake, knowing of our interest through the gift we had sent. All were thrilled to hear him recite specific matters of record that revealed God's hand moving along the exact lines we had prayed about!

That request established our basic stance. A new mood began to govern our praying. We no longer "just prayed." Instead we *defined* our objectives in prayer, *believed* our God would answer, and *served* the situation in any way we could when that was possible.

We also dispensed with the traditional appeal for "unspoken requests." If it should be prayed about, then it should be spoken. Occasionally matters must be described with discretion because of the intimacy involved, but this is not usually the case. The "unspoken" idea got terribly worn in our circles. Generalized requests (praying for the missionaries, praying for all our unsaved loved ones, and so on) were stopped. Now, when we pray for missionaries, we name them. When we pray for unsaved loved ones, we bring particular people before the throne of God.

We renounced the painfully dishonest and lazy habits of evangelical Christendom's "prayer meeting." We sought new and living ways to show that when we prayed, we meant it.

And God heard and answered!

I am sorry now that we have failed to keep a written record of answered prayer. Calls come every week from around the nation and the world, asking this congregation to pray. This is not to our credit, nor do I write these words to commend my own congregation. We are unworthy servants; we have done only what was our duty (Luke 17:10).

Does that seem self-commending? Jesus told us to say it. And the kind of prayer privileges He has given His Church are so clear in His Word, and so dynamic when we exercise them, that we have little reason to be elated with ourselves for assuming a neglected duty.

## Distinct Assignments

It was November 1973. Watergate and Vietnam were wrenching the soul of the United States of America. It was on a Wednesday night during that month that the Holy Spirit engraved upon our hearts the responsibility to pray for our land.

A word of prophecy stirred in my soul as I stood to teach from the Bible. I suddenly saw God's commission and my heart ignited with His passion:

If my people, which are called by my name, shall humble themselves, and pray, and seek my face, and turn from their wicked ways; then will I hear from heaven, and will forgive their sin, and will heal their land.

(II Chronicles 7:14, KJV)

Then I spoke with Holy Spirit anointing in the name of the Lord:

"I am calling this congregation to pray for your nation, and I am calling you to pray as though no other church were praying. I do not say to you that no others *are* praying, but that you are to pray as *though* no others were. If you will keep My word in this matter, I will fulfill My promise."

The word was much longer than that, including much exhortation and a call to repentance, especially because passivity in intercession is characteristic of most of God's people.

Our response was not at all grand. We accepted it, but we knew too little of the meaning and price of true intercession to understand exactly what our response would require.

One of the elders passed me a slip of paper with a Scripture reference on it. The passage was familiar, but at that moment struck me with new force:

I exhort therefore, that, *first of all,* supplications, prayers, intercessions, and giving of thanks, be made for all men; for kings, and for all that are in authority; that we may lead a quiet and peaceable life in all godliness and honesty.

(I Timothy 2:1-2, KJV, italics added)

Not until that moment had I seen it: such praying is a priority for the entire Church! Explicitly, people will enjoy "a quiet and peaceable life" only in a nation for which the Church in that land is praying.

With that, we began a pilgrimage to learn the meaning of intercession—a pilgrimage that continues to this day. Soon after that evening, for several months, we set 7:14 p.m. each Wednesday as a reminder of our national intercessory assignment on the basis of II Chronicles 7:14. Our methods and themes of prayer expanded as we learned together.

One teacher has defined intercession as "Holy Spirit-directed and Holy Spirit-empowered prayer." That is what we learned—to seek and allow the Holy Spirit to show us what to pray for and how to go about it. Just as we had learned more about prayer as a result of that one request concerning the earthquake, so now we were learning new dimensions of prayer every week concerning our nation's life and neediness.

It was at this juncture that the Holy Spirit moved us to do something in addition to prayer as intercessors for the nation. He called us to enlist others in national intercession. Without self-righteousness, we began to reach out in Jesus' name to unite the Church across the nation in emergency prayer.

Two members of our church, Jim and Carol Owens—the renowned and beloved composers who wrote *Come Together* to express what the Holy Spirit had taught us about "threefold ministry"—now felt the Lord directing them to write a musical about intercessory prayer for nations. The result of that prompting was "*If My People . . .*" It led people into intercession so effectively that we began to sense God directing us as a congregation to give "*If My People . . .*" to the nation.

It would require another book to report the agony and ecstasy, the tears and the triumphs of that project. But we sent forth a national touring group—a crew of 50 musicians, singers and technicians—who presented concerts in more than 65 major cities across the United States. Members of our congregation filled key roles in the execution of this herculean task: LaVerne Campbell coordinated the tour; Pat Boone and Dean Jones narrated the teaching in many cities; the Second Chapter of Acts and Jamie Owens-Collins carried lead singing assignments; Bill Braden-McIlvride was advanceman and producer; and Jim and Carol provided leadership for the road troupe.

They sang from the Sports Arena in Los Angeles to the steps of the Capitol in Washington, D.C.; and as they did, our congregation guaranteed the $365,000 budget for the project, six months long in all. As we all stood together, miracles began to take place. Other people rallied to support us as well, and every need was met. Best of all, multitudes responded with abiding commitments to national intercession. A God-given mission and vision had been fulfilled.

What happened as a result? It's impossible to say, but this much is clear. When we began to pray, social and political analysts were saying that the U.S. was undergoing its greatest time of national division and turmoil since the Civil War. Three years later, after the Church in this country had moved to prayer, even the most cynical journalists agreed that "a new spirit" had come to our nation. Some had said that the 1976 Bicentennial celebration might have become our national funeral; but, in fact, we enjoyed a revived national faith and a measure of peace.

I write these words in praise to God.

## Invading the Impossible

One Sunday morning in June 1975, two years after the Lord launched us into intercessory prayer, I began a teaching series on prayer. The theme, "Invading the Impossible," would eventually become the title of a book on the subject, but more memorable to me is that day's message, because of a prophetic utterance that followed the sermon. The wife of one of our elders spoke by the Holy Spirit:

"My people, I have called you before to pray for your land, but this day I call you to a broader field of responsibility that I now give. I will make this place a house of prayer for all nations, and I am calling you as a people in this place to pray for all the nations of the world everywhere."

It took me a full year to understand clearly how that message was to be lived out: we were supposed to pray for *every* nation. The sheer magnitude of it boggled my mind! But by waiting on God, we found a path for this added ministry, and today virtually every nation on earth is sustained before God's throne in prayer by some group in our congregation.

Each "home group" (I'll describe them later) carries an international prayer assignment; and I have asked *every* member of the congregation to ask the Holy Spirit what nation He would have him pray for.

Today, at family prayer times, each person may mention "his" or "her" nation. Some of our people initiate programs of contact with "their" nation. Some have visited the land for which they pray, and others carry on correspondence with missionaries serving there.

In addition, we believe God has assigned us other sorts of prayer responsibilities. We want people who face cancer to have a place of prayer-refuge among us. We deeply believe that yet another youth revival awaits this nation, intended by God to exceed the Jesus Movement of the late '60s and early '70s. We are also committed to pray corporately and constantly for the nations of Israel, England and China.

Why these nations?

1. The Bible teaches that all of us should pray for "the peace of Jerusalem" (Psalm 122:6). This is more than a contrived "love-the-Jews-and-get-excited-about-prophecy" superficiality. It is a responsible point of prayer based on Romans 9-11.
2. England is our land's "parent nation." We pray for her

with a sense that God will bless us the way He blesses children who honor their parents—"that thy days may be long upon the land which the Lord thy God giveth thee" (Exodus 20:12). We believe this may also have national consequences.

3. China is the world's most populous land, and merits our special concern for that alone. In 1976, however, we sensed the voice of the Holy Spirit pointing us toward it. Since that time, we have watched in prayer and gradually seen access to that country reopened, and open church worship reinstituted there. (*Please note:* In recording answers to prayer, we hasten to affirm our confidence that there are many others praying besides our congregation. We *never* take credit for answered prayer; we simply accept the responsibility to pray.)

One way many in the congregation join to fulfill our intercessory assignment is to participate each week in a one-hour prayer watch. We ask that they give the hour completely to prayer for those matters that "The Church On The Way" carries as our God-given concerns.

This practice originated more recently, during our Good Friday Service in 1978. During that service the Holy Spirit impressed Jesus' words deeply upon our hearts: "Could you not watch with me one hour?" (Matthew 26:40). Other times may be given to other matters, but if each member of the congregation will give one hour in this way, we can prove ourselves good soldiers in the spiritual conflict being waged in these days with ferocity. As we do, I am at peace that we are remaining faithful to "pray without ceasing" for those matters the Holy Spirit has assigned to us.

## A Wednesday Night Visit

As I have already said, the three major services of the week follow the same basic patterns I've described. They differ from one another in emphasis, but each generally retains its basic pattern while we allow for the Holy Spirit's improvisation.

Each Wednesday evening at 7:00, I walk out onto the platform of our sanctuary, which we call our "living room." The room is humming with excitement, for the family is together and fellowshiping. I generally make a few remarks to draw the people together, and then we begin singing. We sing praises to God—high praises.

Psalm 149 outlines the privileged authority of saints over the adversaries of Yahweh:

> Let the high praises of God be in their mouth, and a two-edged sword in their hand, to execute vengeance upon the heathen, and punishments upon the enemy; to bind their authorities with chains and fetters of iron; to exact the judgment which has already been written: this honor belongs to the saints of God—Hallelujah!
>
> (Psalm 149:6-9, paraphrase)

As a rule, worship continues for ten or fifteen minutes, usually comprised of a mixture of praise, prayer, and sometimes prophetic utterance. Next we open our Bibles to the text undergirding whatever specific point of national intercession I will address this particular evening. I define and elaborate on how we should press this point in prayer.

Then, for another ten or fifteen minutes, the entire congregation kneels to pray. Each person partners with another, and they pray together for at least part of that time about the matters I have outlined.

This season concludes as we rise in a triumphant declaration in song: "I Exalt Thee," or "Our God Reigns," or "Unto Him Be Glory in the Church." We declare the victory of faith!

Then I invite everyone to greet those around them and enjoy fellowship for the next few minutes. Singing draws us back together to the water baptismal service (one is conducted almost every Sunday and Wednesday evening). We rejoice to witness those who are submitting to the Lordship of Jesus Christ in this way.

Next we focus on some area of ministry. Usually I teach about it, and I may invite other people to the platform to help in some way. They may testify about a victory of faith they have enjoyed. Or they may come because they are going out from us to serve elsewhere, and we want to commission them and assure them of our prayers. Or they may come because they symbolize a special point of prayer that should concern the whole assembly.

The congregation then stands again and forms small circles to pray over the matter just discussed. At this time, we distribute prayer request cards among the circles. On the cards are various personal concerns that people have called or written in.

We employ various means to ensure that the scores of cards are prayed over. At times, we mention none publicly but distribute them by hand into prayer circles. At other times, we read a few for the whole assembly to hear, and distribute the balance. On rare occasions I have taken time to read through the entire number of as many as 40 specific requests.

As we listen, I often pause to suggest how we might learn to pray for different matters. Irrespective of how many we pray for in the service, we put all the cards afterward into the prayer room, where intercessors will continue that week to attend to them.

By this time, an hour has passed almost without notice. Then, for 35-45 minutes, I usually teach some expositional or thematic series.

It is drawing near 9:00. The children in the nursery and the "Kids of the Kingdom" are now awaiting their parents. I dismiss and commission the people: "Love one another, Church!"

Nearly two hours have gone by. The world is changing because of what has gone on here. The Holy Spirit of intercession is a Spirit of travail; and where we travail in prayer, life comes forth and the Kingdom of God extends its triumph over the works of darkness.

# Chapter 10

# RELEASING A MAN'S POTENTIAL

If I were forced to choose which regular service or event at "The Church On The Way" I would place highest in my own schedule, I could do so without hesitation. The monthly Men's Growth Seminar is, to my mind, the single most important thing that happens each month in this congregation.

I may be accused of devaluing corporate worship or of a chauvinistic deference to men, but I am willing to risk those miscalculations, because both the experience and the Word verify the practical wisdom of giving first place to training men.

Jesus did. In fact, He poured the preponderance of His time into training the Twelve. The sum total of His public ministry could not begin to equal the aggregate result of His input into those disciples who lived and traveled with Him over the short years of His public ministry.

The New Testament gives sufficient priority to discipling men to warrant this as a requirement of all pastoral leadership. The words of II Timothy 2:2 provide the pathway to loosing new leadership for the Church: "And the things that thou hast heard of me among many witnesses, the same commit thou to faithful men, who shall be able to teach others also" (KJV).

What the blood of Christ is to salvation, and what the Holy Spirit's outpouring is to enabling, so the training of men is to the release of leadership for the Church.

By leadership I am speaking not only of pastors, missionaries and the like. I mean leaders in the home, in business, in the community; leaders in character, in moral influence, in finance; and only coincidentally leaders in the Church.

Furthermore, I do not mean only male leaders. God wants to release leadership through women as well. I do not hold with any who deny the influence of a woman's leadership, but I am at once persuaded that her full capacity cannot be discovered apart from men who recognize and serve their role in God's creative and redemptive order.

It is at this point that possibility for misunderstanding exists.

## The Man's Place in Redemption

Widespread confusion reigns over the question of the relative places of man and woman in God's present economy. Let me emphasize that word *present*, since God deals presently with things that are not as initially created, nor as they ultimately will be.

In the created order, man was made male and female with a coequal status of full partnership in their God-given dominion over all of earth. The dead traditions distilling from ignorant interpretations of the King James rendering of Genesis 2:18—"And the Lord God said, It is not good that the man should be alone; I will make him a helpmeet for him"—have consistently demeaned the woman as a "helpmeet," a seeming synonym for a second party or inferior. The precise meaning of the text would disclose God's creative intent more accurately: "I will make a partner designed to complement and precisely suit the man."

Nothing here implies a reduced role of privilege or influence. The word *complement* indicates man's dependence upon woman for his own completion—her equal role with him in fulfilling God's assignment to replenish, subdue and have dominion over the earth. A mutuality of relationship is suggested at every dimension of their being; and no biblical grounds exist for making woman anything other than a joint participant with man in all of life.

The redemptive order introduces God's plan toward restoring this lost equality. Scripture declares the intent of full and equal partnership, but it remains today for men and women to regain that partnering relationship only on specific and biblical terms. Male and female are damaged through the fall of mankind, and now, together in sin, their togetherness in life is a broken ideal.

But where redeemed men and women accept redemption's terms of growth toward the rediscovery of that lost equality and partnership, it becomes a realizable goal. Those terms are expressed in words that annoy some people. They require faith and trust to live out. The idea of "submission," and words such as "headship" and "order," must be confronted, and their livability learned in the spirit of truth and love.

Put simply, the Bible teaches that the fall of man altered the grounds on which equal partnership could be realized. Those original grounds were simple: Life *was* that way. Mankind, male and female, was created that way. Woman was made an equal partner; and that was that.

But sin marred them both, destroying the beauty of the first order until a new order would make recovery possible. The challenge facing us today in man-woman relationships is to learn how married partners may learn and grow into the harmony, unity and partnership that the Scriptures show. The way is in the redemptive order Christ has brought through the new creation (II Corinthians 5:17). His cross releases power for the restoration of man and woman in the divine ideal, but that realization requires time—and growth.

Unlike the created order, which was the pristine product of God's precise shaping of things in His divine image and intent, the redemptive order is a process. Recovery is not instantaneous, as things were in the created order.

In all of the believer's life, a dynamic tension exists between the individual's present maturity and the image of Christ that

God wills for his full maturity. This gap between what a believer is and what he is called to become in Christ creates the misunderstanding that surrounds the theme of man-woman and husband-wife roles and relationships. A bridge cannot be built over that gap by doctrinaire ideas—only by personal growth.

No thinking person would try to justify the grotesque misappropriations of the word *submission*. Domestic, commercial, political and ecclesiastical relationships are riddled with examples of human exploitation and manipulation, in which "submission" is defined as one party having "authority" over the other.

One element of authority, properly understood, is inherent in the idea of submission. The primary concept refers, not to leaders wielding authority over others, but to people who accept divinely arranged order *for the sake of protection, fulfillment and realization.*

A citizen's submission to government, for example, is intended in God's order, but not to grant the rise of a ruling class who lord it over the population. God gives political leadership to serve the multitudes and to release the maximum possibilities for each citizen. When any government fails this ideal, it is not God's fault. Someday He shall call all nations to account for their use or abuse of power. Leaders in government need redemptive understanding in order to bless their citizens.

## How Submission Works

A ready biblical example demonstrates best the intent of submission as an idea: the example of Christ and His Church. The Lordship and sovereign rulership of Jesus Christ is unquestioned with reference to His Church. He has saved us by dying for us. He has risen and asserted His power over all things. He is worthy of our bowed knee, and we willingly submit to Him as Savior and Lord, for His surrender of Himself in our interests has won our trust—our submission to His leadership.

The awesome truth about this relationship is that He is committed ultimately to bring His redeemed to a place of joint-heirship with Him—absolutely full and equal partnership (Romans 8:16-17). His process of redemption is toward our progress in grace. His goal is our equal partnership with Him, "reigning in life" (Romans 5:17). But the incredible privilege of sharing equally with the King of the universe in His rule is granted on specific terms: that we relearn God's order through a submitted relationship to Him as our Head, the Source of life's stream to us.

It is through this basic truth—the relationship between Christ and His Church—that rediscovery of man's and woman's relationship and privileges is taught in Scripture.

Two passages establish the parallel: I Corinthians 11:1-16 and Ephesians 5:21-33. Both deal with husband-to-wife or man-to-woman relationships. Without qualification, both passages make the man the key to the release of the redemptive process for them both. While either married partner may be saved independently of the other, what happens in the man's true growth will determine the degree to which the richness of the original creative order can be recovered in their relationship.

Nothing in the redemptive order places man over woman as a dominator, but as a servant dedicated to woman's fulfillment. Like Christ for the Church, man's role is to be "savior of the body" of their union—a task requiring the development of Christ's loving, serving ways in the man. Nonetheless, distortion and confusion have corrupted these texts, due to both man's carnality and woman's fear.

With the conviction that building men is the only way to realize the Lord's goal for happy homes, well-trained children, recovered relationships and people's increasing maturity, I began our Men's Ministries in 1972. An encounter with the Holy Spirit while I was in Illinois that February burned these words on my heart:

*Begin to meet with the men, and I will raise up elders and servants to accomplish My purpose here.*

I issued an invitation to the men of the congregation, and buttressed it with a personal letter to about 35 of them: "I'm asking you to meet with me that I might bare my heart concerning something I believe God would like to do in you . . . and in me."

A nucleus of about 30 gathered the first time, and a pattern to the monthly meetings began to emerge. Since I was convinced that all of life flows from worshiping before God's throne, I would lead the men in openhearted song and praise. This provided many opportunities to confront the supposition that forthright spirituality is not truly masculine—that the supposedly mystical nature of spiritual pursuit is better confined to the intuitive approach of the woman.

I would base my leadership of the men in worship on scriptural examples of wholehearted "I love God" examples such as David, Jacob, Peter, Abraham, Paul, Samuel and John. The biblical picture shows men of complete devotion; but those men of spiritual sensitivity are also seen as warriors, wrestlers, rugged fishermen, adventurers, pioneers, and men unafraid to face life-and-death situations. Manliness is obviously not inconsistent with open and forthright spirituality and unabashed, outspoken worship. Devotion to God is demonstrated as being the fountainhead to the fullest realization of true masculinity.

After worship, I would direct the men in interaction. I would describe a particular masculine problem or concern, and illustrate the case with a transparent confession of my own temptation, fear, weakness or doubt in that area.

Sharing together in powerful, supportive prayer began to become a practice as men learned the liberty of openly acknowledging their own hearts. Transparent communication breeds refinement of character and honesty in relationships. "Iron sharpens iron, and so a man sharpens the countenance of his friend" (Proverbs 27:17).

These times do not require the dredging of distant failures,

as though we were seeking emotional or psychological cathar-
sis. In fact, we emphasize that the past is cleansed by Calvary,
and condemnation covered by Jesus' blood.

But these times have proven to be dynamic as men "sharp-
en" one another by openly relating points of stress and need in
their personal lives. Current trials or definite points of temptation to sin are brought into focus; fear and doubt are confronted in faith; and brother joins with brother as partners in
battle.

I am not so naive as to suppose that every man shares his
deepest need with full transparency, or that this interaction
time covers every point on the spectrum of sin's pressure
against those gathered in fellowship. But I know it establishes
a beginning, and over the years has manifested its fruitfulness
in a growing body of men who would entrust their lives to one
another.

Society implies that a man's strength is in his own self-
determinism, rugged individualism or macho masculinity. In
our times of interaction, we affirm from the Word of God, and
then practice in partnership, certain powerful concepts: that
"two are better than one . . . . and a threefold cord is not
quickly broken" (Ecclesiastes 4:9, 12); that "if two of you shall
agree . . ." (Matthew 18:19); that "none of us lives unto himself or dies unto himself" (Romans 14:7); and that we are to
"bear . . . one another's burdens and so fulfill the law of
Christ" (Galatians 6:2).

The third part of each of our Men's Seminars involves an
extended period of teaching. The objective is always to address some truth in the Word of God, by which I do one of four
things:

1. Speak to those facets of society's influence on a man
   that claim to enhance his manhood, but that actually
   emasculate and reduce him into the world's image
   (thus, economic, commercial, ideological and philo-
   sophical influences are identified and countered);

2. Confront those specific influences that most erode a man's spiritual base of confidence before God (e.g., impurity of mind, sexual fantasy, corrupt language, deteriorated relationships, preoccupation with "things"—covetousness, avarice, etc.);
3. Emphasize the grounds of confidence in Christ's victory within, through underscoring redemption's triumph over sin in the flesh; rising above condemnation; the Holy Spirit's fullness as an immediate and abiding availability to each man; and the resources of the Word on a practical, applicable basis;
4. Build the individual through a deepened perspective on his own calling, and gifts for ministering the life and Kingdom of Jesus Christ through the unique, creative agency of his own innate, God-given abilities.

By these four means, a man comes to recognize enemies to his growth, along with his resources for maturity and ministry.

As years have passed, God has multiplied not only the number of men involved (over 1,200 at this writing, with an average of 800 present every month); He has developed strong men who assist in the teaching of the others.

Now I speak to all the men only in a general session that begins each seminar. A program of multiphased development awaits each man entering at the first-year level. A complete three-year program is outlined in three ten-month phases (seminars do not convene July and August). The stated objectives, curricular plan and explicit goals are published like this:

Our Men's Growth Seminar is a monthly (first Friday night) three-hour session designed to develop a man for spiritual influence and leadership. The objectives are:

1. To establish the man who has made up his mind to let

God make him all that he can become, according to the Father's purpose for his life.

2. To enlarge a man's understanding of himself, his responsibilities as a man, a husband, a friend and a servant of Jesus Christ.
3. To expel from men's minds the false concepts of masculinity which hinder the freedom of the individual to function in true spiritual authority.
4. To engage men at a spiritual commitment level which will release his individual capacity for genuine transparency and faithful relationship.

The curriculum is three years, each constituted of two five-month sessions. Beside these teaching sessions, retreats serve as times of total interaction of the whole body of men—also ideal times for incorporating new men into the flow of the men's seminar life and spirit.

### Year I

Man Alive!

*Release* of the soul; focus on understanding the nature of worldmindedness upon men and the pathway of freedom.

Middle-Man

Instruction in the structure of God's order in all *relationships*, and the biblical response to each arena of responsibility.

### Year II

Man-Power

Instruction in the *resources* available in the Spirit-filled life, and how to move in that dimension of experience constantly.

| Man-Word | Guidance in the individual's use of God's Word; how to receive its *revelation* through both study and prophetic insight. |

*Year III*

| Man-Makers | Learning to *disciple other men* through an availability to partnership; understanding the principles of life-investment. |

| Man-Movers | Learning to *lead* in group situations, home settings, family gatherings, etc. Basic principles of developing group ministries. |

Explicit goals:

1. To have specific entry and exit points in the men's ministry program. (The completion of this course should at least qualify a man to lead or partner in leading small groups within the congregation.)
2. To point a way for men to move toward personal freedom, personal development and personal effectiveness as a believer, and as a functioning part of his congregation;
3. To focus on the need for men prepared for ministry in the Body, and to provide a clearly defined channel for pursuing such preparation.

These published objectives are circulated widely at the end of summer and the beginning of the calendar year. I consider as one of my primary pastoral duties the recruitment of new men into the seminars. My task is greatly simplified, however, by the readiness with which men invite others once they have tasted the joy and fulfillment of growing in true, Bible-based manhood.

There is no question as to the fruit of this pursuit. It is biblically based and spiritually alive. It attracts men. It builds men and qualifies them for leadership.

The result is twofold: First, we have hundreds of homes that have begun to learn God's order; and there are wives everywhere in our congregation who marvel at the release in their husbands, and the ensuing release in their own and their children's lives.

One wife wrote me as follows:

> I felt it would bless you, Pastor Jack, to hear how your ministry to the men has been working in Jim's and my personal lives. The meetings Jim attends at Men's Growth are always special and I look forward to his sharing with me whatever the Lord teaches him.
>
> I wanted to confirm to you that the Men's Growth Seminars are filtering through to the rest of the families represented in attendance. I'm an example.
>
> Because of your faithful commitment to teach our men and through the faithfulness and open heart of my sweet husband to receive, I've been healed, delivered, set free—whatever you want to name it—and it's all just happening. Some mornings I wake up knowing God has been healing me in my sleep. And do I have ears to hear and eyes to see!

So one sees how, as men grow, the congregation begins to be filled with dynamic women discovering their true opportunity to *become*. Women have a voice and influence in our church, which is scripturally ordered and sweetly yet powerfully communicated.

Women at "The Church On The Way" are liberated, but they aren't mad about it. Christ's way of liberation, through freeing men who lovingly serve and release the women they influence, is both beautiful and beautifying; and our women are examples of it. They are increasingly beautiful—in their strength, communication, appearance, management, skill at serving, conduct of their homes, work in the community, accomplishment on their jobs, leadership in society, and witness for Jesus Christ.

A second benefit of the men's seminars is our harvest of leadership for rising ministries in the church. Our home groups, our teachers, our usher body, our music ministries, our youth workers and so on—all these are enhanced and even made possible through the increased availability of people who are learning their purpose and identity, and can now help others find theirs.

We would have not been able to respond as quickly, for example, to the Holy Spirit's prompting to home ministries development a few years ago were it not for the fact that the Holy Spirit had moved upon me several years before that: *Begin to meet with the men, and I will raise up elders and servants to accomplish My purpose here.*

I did. And He did.

And I'm glad!

# Chapter 11

# MEETING HOUSE TO HOUSE

During rush hour, the Shinjuku commuter terminal in Tokyo is a cross between an anthill, a NASA Space Center countdown and the Indianapolis 500. While trains shake the ground, rumbling up to the station's multiple platforms, each car stops just in time to belch forth a cluster of humanity that forms a phalanx and moves toward the ramps and doorways leading to work via the street or another train.

What ingenuity, combined with a penchant for regimentation and synchronization, to pick up and deliver over two million passengers per business day at one site! And it is done every single workday at Shinjuku.

One day in April 1977, I stood against a sidewall of one of the tunnels through which droves of Japanese humanity were flowing, within speaking distance of more than 25,000 people who passed me in less than a quarter of an hour.

Aside from the other things that impressed me—the efficiency of management, the precision timing, the coordination of crowd direction and control—I was most moved to see the sheer mass of humanity moving through the terminal, and the unique blend of intensity and delicacy manifested in these remarkable people.

I was in Japan at the request of Team Thrust Ministries, speaking daily to groups of pastors who came to major cities in which conferences were held. I had come to Shinjuku, however, as a tourist. And here my heart began to throb with a sense of the Holy Spirit moving. Somehow I felt the heart of God for these multitudes.

I didn't have a vision. I didn't hear any words. I didn't talk with one person. But I had an experience. Later it occurred to me that I may have felt something that Jesus felt:

> But when he saw the multitudes, he was moved with compassion on them, because they fainted, and were scattered abroad, as sheep having no shepherd.
>
> (Matthew 9:36, KJV)

Matthew reports that, as a consequence of that experience, Jesus did two things. First, He told His disciples to pray the Lord of the harvest to send laborers into the field, because the harvest was plentiful and there was a shortage of harvesters. Second, He took men who had been in training with Him and commissioned them to broader ministry.

That day in Tokyo was the pivotal point in bringing about our Home Ministries Department at "The Church On The Way." We had spent several years helping the people of my flock to see themselves as ministers and to develop their leadership potential. Now, it seemed, the Holy Spirit was probing to see how seriously we would follow this course.

We had to face and acknowledge the impossibility of ministering adequately to the multitudes of humanity by traditional methods. And we needed to take a new step in trusting the Holy Spirit to work in and through the people I had trained.

I cannot say I was moved with a burden for Japan or any other people in particular. I simply felt a concern for *masses*, multitudes everywhere, the earth's billions. When the Church tries to reach mankind, we tend to be building-oriented. Our objective becomes "bringing the crowd in." But analysts have shown that even if every church building in the world were filled several times every Sunday, only a pitifully small percentage of mankind could be accommodated.

In our own San Fernando Valley, if every religious facility were filled four times every week with a different group each time, less than half the one-and-a-quarter-million people in our own section of greater Los Angeles could be served.

If we were concerned only with evangelization, the answer to this problem might be mass media—literature, radio, television. However, Jesus did not commission the Church only to evangelize. The Church is to reach, disciple and shepherd. And no one can adequately disciple or fully shepherd by radio waves, a tube, celluloid or the finest literature.

I am too involved in these multiple approaches to discount the many evangelistic agencies in the Church at large that employ the media effectively, seeking to touch the masses. But everyone who is evangelized needs to receive fellowship and pastoral care. It is one thing to reach people with a touch, and quite another to embrace them in God's love.

I realized in 1977 that "The Church On The Way" had to expand its horizons if we, as one congregation, were to be what God wanted us to be in our small segment of this giant globe. We had to break any mentality still residing among us that might see our building—the home base—as anything more than the central gathering place for the congregation. The offices that serviced the body, and the living room where the family gathered, must not become the primary focus of our thought. The center of our operations dared not become the center of our vision!

Yet to expand our circle of ministry would require a dramatic increase in leadership. We would need to release scores more men and women to perform work usually reserved for professional clergy. And actually, that wasn't unthinkable. Many people were trained and ready to go. Some were already working in ministry. The obstacle was in deciding to do it on a large scale.

I had to reach a decision, and so did they. I would have to decide if I would truly trust them. They would have to decide if they would accept the trust faithfully. People of the flock would be making deepened commitments, investing trust in men and women who would care for them much closer to home than I could. These new workers would teach and counsel and exhort from the Word of God.

And the Holy Spirit was asking me to decide: *Will you trust Me to work in people as you have taught them to expect Me to?*

I had heard of home group ministries before, of course. In fact, we already had a fellowship group program of a sort. But what the Holy Spirit was now pressing into my heart was unlike anything I had heard. The entire congregation had to be involved. This could be no optional "home fellowship" program. Also, it had to occupy a place in the congregation's life that clearly indicated its priority. So we started to work to accomplish these two things.

First, I shared my heart with the pastoral staff and the elders, and they confirmed what I felt. Then, in the May and June Men's Growth Seminars, I taught on the theme "Ministry to the Multitudes." I told the men how and why I needed to release hundreds of them to new levels of responsibility in leadership.

Also in June, I taught a series of lessons to the congregation on the same theme. Here is a sampling of the texts we studied that May and June, which helped convince us all that this was not just my idea, but something the Holy Spirit wanted:

And they, continuing daily with one accord in the temple, and breaking bread from house to house . . . .

(Acts 2:46, KJV)

And daily in the temple, and in every house, they ceased not to teach and preach Jesus Christ.

(Acts 5:42, KJV)

. . . And how I kept back nothing that was profitable unto you, but have showed you, and have taught you publicly, and from house to house . . . .

(Acts 20:20, KJV)

In the Scriptures, the cultivation of ministry by believers in homes did not nullify the place or authority of God-ordained leaders who oversaw it all. While meeting "from house to house," there remained a central commitment, even as the first-century Christians were "daily in the temple."

But home meetings have had a checkered history among many church groups in the United States, often culminating in disorder, fanaticism, immorality or division. Some of our staff, aware of this, were guarded about the subject, though they did not oppose the experiment. And their reservations made sense. If a home group became a law unto itself, or if its ministry moved out from under a place of submission to the whole congregation, then the body could be torn.

But we felt reasonably secure in the balance taught by Scripture, in which the base of fellowship holds its satellites in proper orbit.

It was at this time that God gave a prophetic vision to one of our leaders. He saw an old-fashioned wagon wheel rolling forward. He noticed in particular the hub, spokes and rim; and the Holy Spirit seemed to show him that "the wheel moves forward smoothly because it is attached firmly to the hub, and because the spokes keep an even distance between the hub and the rim."

We noted three important things: first, that the hub (the home base, the congregation's center of operation) must be strong. This strength is not found in its domination but in its service and coordination. A wheel is oiled at the hub; and accordingly, we saw another picture of the concept of submission, in which anointing flows from the head.

Second, we noted that the spokes—the connections between the hub and the rim—must be even in length. We must maintain a consistency in the approach, style and content of ministry between the home meeting and the home base. Instruction, communication and similarity of operation to the home meeting would do this.

Third, we noted that the rim—the perimeter on which the wheel rolls forward—was like the home groups themselves.

Interestingly, the vision shows that the unity is as complete at the end of the spokes as at the hub, for the whole wheel becomes a complete circle again.

The picture was a powerful message in itself, for it helped us to see that God was gearing us for a new season when He would expand our call to be "on the way."

Our problem remained—how to demonstrate this home ministry as a corporate priority. To do that, we had to accept a challenge. When would the home groups meet? The selection of the day and hour would determine the degree of importance the congregation would attach to home groups. We wanted the message to be loud and clear.

Accordingly, we set the time: Sunday mornings. No time is more important to the life of a church than that! And, realistically, no time is more crucial to its financial life—a fact that pastors outside our congregation have underscored when they make observations about the plan we felt necessary to establish the importance of our home groups.

I proposed that every home group would meet once each month on a Sunday morning, and once each month at another time of their selection. Each of these two meetings would have a separate purpose. The Sunday meeting would be a replica of a regular Sunday worship gathering at the home base. The alternate meeting would be an occasion for fellowship to develop a sense of community and interaction. We differentiated between these two gatherings in this way:

1. *Worshiping together,* Sunday morning, once a month. The times we gather on the Lord's Day are essentially times of knowing and growing: knowing the Father through worship, and growing in Jesus through the Word (Psalm 46:10; II Peter 3:18).

2. *Fellowshiping together,* monthly, wherever each group wishes. The times we gather for activities other than worship and teaching are times of sharing and caring: sharing through testimony of what the Lord Jesus is

doing in our lives, and caring through providing help, encouragement or practical aid to those in personal, spiritual or material need (Acts 2:44-47; Revelation 12:ll).

As I mentioned, we had a fellowship group program of a sort before this full-scale launch into home groups. We had attempted to involve every member in a fellowship group of approximately 50 people who lived in the same vicinity. This had worked reasonably well. Now, however, things were different. The congregation had to know we were into home ministries "for keeps." I prepared a memo to the people and read it in each of the Sunday services:

The greatest challenge ever to our flexibility as a congregation will be the morning of *August 14, 1977*. On that day no *morning* services will be held here. The purpose of this plan is to experience an approach which will become a way of life every month. Beginning mid-September, each month the congregation will be asked to attend their home meeting on the Sunday morning specified. Thus, one quarter of the congregation will meet in home groups each Sunday. *The objective is threefold:*

1. We believe there are dimensions of true New Testament life that cannot be tested or profitably gained apart from deeper developments than we have yet learned in small group involvement.

These developments involve both fellowship and leadership. As a congregation committed to developing *ministry* in people, we must be consistent in our practice with the content of our principles. Ministry *to* each other will be cultivated at a more demanding dimension; ministry *through* maturing leadership will be released to new possibilities.

2. We believe the Bible clearly shows that the New Testament church was as effective in home gatherings on the perimeter of its life as it was in larger gatherings at the center of its life. The biblical congregation is not dependent upon its larger gatherings for the *exercise* of its ministry; nor is it independent of its central leadership in the direction of its ministry. The healthy corporate body learns to move with force and flexibility, but always coordinated under God-given leadership and spiritual authority.

3. We believe that the Holy Spirit has moved us to accept a larger responsibility for *ministry to the* multitudes of people who have no real, comfortable concept of what it is like to be exposed to the Lord, His Word in action, and the love which the Holy Spirit communicates. The only way in which such ministry can be brought to them, and they be led into a trusting fellowship in the context of the larger church situation, is for that ministry to be set in the unthreatening atmosphere of a home.

Such is neither a deceptive approach to them, nor is it a bypassing of biblical authority. To the contrary, it communicates a direct presentation of our spirit, and it presents authority in the way the Scriptures always do—in a spirit of love and a quest for serving.

On *August 14,* we plan to conduct Home Group Meetings at some 200 locations in the Valley and throughout the greater Los Angeles area. These will be our first such meetings in the history of our congregation. It will be a beginning of something that will continue with us into the indefinite future. It is what begins in these meetings that we will learn to refine, develop and extend. These gatherings will meet at 9:45 until *about 11:15 a.m.* Everyone will be learning together. We don't expect perfection, but we do know we will experience progress.

I continued with a second page, reading the memo that was in everyone's hand:

Now, what will be involved in a Home Group Meeting?

| | |
|---|---|
| 9:30-9:45 a.m.<br>Arrival Time | People will be gathering. Name pins provided to help us all know each other. Casual conversation begins around simple themes. "But I have a hard time mixing in such a situation!" Answer: "Fear not. Take up your 'hard time' and walk!" |
| 9:45 a.m.<br>Worship the Lord | The Home Group Leader will have directed you to a reasonably comfortable seating arrangement, and worship time will begin. You won't have the usual instrumental support in most cases, but come on and sing anyway. "The Church On The Way" has never moved on the basis of its niftiness, but on the basis of our commitment. Worship! Helpful to note: You will have a copy of our bulletin for the day. ("Whew! There's *something* I can lean on!") Simple chorus sheets will be provided, too. You're "on the way." |
| Living in<br>the Word | On your chorus sheet, there is a passage of Scripture. We are going to read it. In order to minister to children, our Home Group Meetings (which will involve five-year-olds and up; younger ones will be cared for in another room) will ask everyone to share together in the reading of a Bible story, then to gather in groups of three or four—children included—and retell the story, and what it means. |

| | |
|---|---|
| A few minutes later | The Home Group Leader will invite you to open your Bible with him. (None in the rack—bring your own!) A few words based on Scripture will pave the way into *Ministrytime*—a "Church On The Way" indispensable. One special note: Ministrytime in Home Group Meetings will allow an opportunity for a little more direct interaction. It's a good chance to have one or two give praise reports of answered prayer. We overcome by the word of our testimony (Rev. 12:ll). |
| Let's sing again | "The Church On The Way" sings a lot. Same here in the homes. You can't sit there non-participatively. Sing! "But I sing so badly!" Answer: "Then apologize to the Lord for it, but sing!" |
| Studying the Word | We are all accustomed to outlines. You'll have one, but it will be mostly blank—ready to be filled in as the Home Group Leader shares from his heart and from the Word of God. He will teach for 15-20 minutes, and there may be some time for interactive response—always on a positive theme! (Rule: no preachiness by any of us, only life-to-life sharing!) |
| The Lord's Table | Our fellowship will be complete by our partaking of Communion together. We expect the Lord to be among us, distributing the richness of His life as we distribute the elements "in remembrance of Him." |
| Giving and Blessing Each Other | We will receive tithes and offerings. Each Home Group Leader has been instructed how to transfer the gifts to the offices here. Needless to say, each Home Group Leader is trained and trusted in all that we're doing. |

And with that, lay hands on one another and declare the blessing of God on each other as you go.

The vision of the real "happening" fixed in their minds, it was easier for the people to come to terms with the holy mandate I felt we had been issued. Together we began to gird up for August 14th. We trained scores of couples in four special sessions, preparing them to handle the first meeting. Their participation in this one event did not require them to continue leading a home group, but we asked them to listen to God. The experience might prove to be the Lord's way of inaugurating them into a new ministry in their own homes.

On Sunday, August 14, our home base on Sherman Way was almost as quiet as a tomb. Only a few members of our pastoral staff were there to meet visitors and any others who were either uninformed or had forgotten. They explained what was happening and gave directions to home meetings located nearby with a cordial invitation to join in.

When the congregation gathered all together that night, the atmosphere was electrified! Testimonies abounded. Blessing prevailed. God's people were tasting a new sense of responsibility for and availability to ministry.

Today, the Home Ministries Department of our church holds a high priority. We have no choice, if we are to be the congregation God has called us to be. I feel this so strongly that occasionally I tell the congregation:

"If you have become part of this congregation and you are not part of a home group, I must gently insist that you do something about that very soon. Go to a home to grow, to be stretched as a person, and to serve the Body of Christ. Perhaps you will feel uncomfortable. Don't worry. Visit another home group. You will find a home group suited to you. Begin at once to find that group the Holy Spirit has prepared for you."

At this writing we still feel very "green" in experience, but we are geared; the wheel is turning. The hub is functional, and on the perimeter thousands of the faithful are learning a new dimension of New Testament lifestyle. We are "at home" together, and we are set to serve the multitudes.

# Chapter 12

# CARING FOR THE LAMBS

Children have been too often the victims of revival. While the teenagers and collegians may be stirred to high and lofty ideals, lifelong commitments with deep meaning and noble purpose, the little ones—the infants, preschoolers and pre-teenagers—often suffer.

It is ironic that a people who worship a Man who said, "Allow the children to come unto Me and do nothing to forbid them," can inadvertently, in the midst of the glorious working of the Holy Spirit, become as insensitive as we sometimes do.

In my travels, I have occasionally witnessed small children being corralled into an undersized room, parked in oversized chairs and subjected to an adult-length film on a theme outside their interest or grasp, *while . . .*

In a sanctuary or auditorium designed for their comfort, the adults praise God, fellowship with true spiritual joy, sing hymns with variety and taste, are moved by gifted singers presenting enjoyable music, and are taught by an anointed messenger of the Lord who addresses a theme pertinent to their lives in an interesting way that is also personally transforming.

I have known times and places in which the nursery, designed theoretically for infants under two years old, is a former storage room without windows or ventilation, crowded with a dozen toddlers and crawlers, and more babes-in-arms than the sum of the adult arms in the room is able to tend. Moreover, the room is stifling, smelly and echoing with the sound of crying.

Those who serve in such a setting are gradually injected with a sense of futility that builds to indifference and ends in resentment. Elsewhere in the same building, adults laugh at the quips or weep at the moving testimony of the guest speaker who has attracted so large a crowd that the children's facilities are seriously overloaded. These adults will blithely praise, pray and promote another "successful" occasion, believing that in this way God will bring many souls to Christ.

Since God's grace *does* bring many to new birth despite this unwitting insensitivity on the part of the adults, people misinterpret His blessing as His endorsement. God does not approve such failure to attend properly to the little ones, but His mercy is so great that He overlooks much and still bestows blessing.

I make these observations with a relatively peaceful conscience, for the children's ministry at "The Church On The Way" works today with a considerably higher degree of love and care. Our staff, facilities and supplies all show this. But I cannot be self-righteous. For if God had not worked miraculously and sovereignly to keep us from such neglect, we might ourselves be missing the mark, as we once did and as some others continue to do.

Our story, like so many church mushroom-growth stories, is fraught with the frustrations that occur inevitably when the facilities can scarcely accommodate the number of people who want, and try, to use them. God is never shortsighted, but we often are. We can be so bent on growth that we plan inadequately and erect sloppy organizational structures. God does not honor this, and it gives the enemy many footholds of attack.

Sometimes the way we treat the infants, toddlers and preschoolers almost hearkens back to the child sacrifices of Baal worship, against which the biblical writers inveighed so strongly.

Of course, no congregation *intends* to neglect its children. Nor is it easy to solve all the problems of rapid growth perfectly. Nevertheless, we must at all costs care for our children lovingly, consistently, conscientiously and effectively.

"The Church On The Way" has done that, but not without a pointed word from the Lord.

## First, A Fold for Lambs

It was March 1977, and plans were in full swing to build a new sanctuary. We were leaping hurdles one by one—acquiring lots, advancing preliminary drawings, watching our expectancy rise high. We could almost taste the sweet reality of having a new building in which we could grow and expand our ministry.

I sat down at my desk one morning, and lying on top of everything arranged for my attention was a note from the director of our children's department. I opened it.

> Dear Pastor Jack,
>
> You know my personal commitment to you and the church, and that I would never say or do anything intentionally out-of-order or with a bad attitude. I do not want to sound pushy or be unsubmissive, and so I can only offer these words to you—submitted in the trust that the Holy Spirit will confirm them to you.
>
> While I was at prayer yesterday, particularly as I prayed concerning our plans for the new building, the Lord stopped me and spoke to me. He said, "I will not allow this congregation to build another house until they first prepare a place to correctly care for their lambs."
>
> I don't know what to do about this, but I knew I had to present it to you. I hope this doesn't seem presumptuous.

I sat there at my desk, stunned into a new level of sanity about priorities. It was not that we were guilty of gross neglect. The fact that Anna and I had four children of our own kept the subject much on our minds.

But my eyes misted when I saw something. We were planning for a spacious sanctuary, but had skimped on our plans for the children's facilities. They were being increased at only a fraction of the amount of space being increased for the adult congregation.

Most uncanny of all was the fact that none of us had noticed our ineptitude or the deficiency in our planning. I simply— no, *we* simply hadn't seen it. The children could not readily speak for themselves; and we had not invited any children to our planning sessions! So in our church, the little ones were enduring neglect, as is the lot of children everywhere.

Now God had spoken for them, to tell us we weren't building properly with reference to our *whole* congregation.

We had done *something*, of course. In fact, we felt we had done much. We had purchased two apartment houses—a total of 24 units—and gained temporary permission to use them as classrooms. And we did have outstanding leaders—a committed and skilled, dedicated and trained group of people who coordinated and carried out our program to care for and teach the children. We had a well-organized nursery, and we were careful to service and maintain the facilities.

But there it was, an incredible and memorable fact: although we were planning to increase the sanctuary area by about 300 percent, we discovered that we were planning to increase the children's space by less than 75 percent.

I took the director's note to the pastoral staff meeting. After I read it, silence reigned. They were, as I had been, stunned.

A few days later, I met with the church council—the elders who govern the business affairs of the congregation—and their response was identical. We all felt more enlightened than we did called to repent. We had not actually failed our children, but had been on the brink of failure and rescued by the prompting of the Holy Spirit.

I still marvel at how our attempts to handle church growth nearly overlooked the future of the church: His children. We took immediate action to remedy this oversight and gave hearty thanks to God for saving us from ourselves.

Since this episode, I have seen something new in Peter's encounter with Jesus beside the Sea of Galilee (John 21). Jesus first told him, "Feed my lambs." Next He said, twice, "Feed my sheep." But He clearly called Peter first to care for *lambs*. He taught us the same thing.

## Nursery Ministry

While this event emphasized the priority of our children's ministry, we had begun long since to learn a pattern of service to our young.

We had first had to decide how we would serve the little ones within days of our arrival in Van Nuys. When Anna and I brought our eleven-month-old infant to the nursery, the facilities were exhausted immediately. You see, one couple with a baby was there already, and the nursery could accommodate only two.

However, space was available for expansion. We had a dozen classrooms and only two Sunday school classes! So I arranged to convert two adjoining classrooms into a pleasant, functional site where families could come and rest their infants. Although funds were limited, we hired a professional nurse to watch over the children during services; and for the first year this plan served us well. It allowed all the mothers to be in the meetings so that everyone could grow together. When the same women are in the nursery constantly, they miss out on the inspiration of Body life. We were glad to be able to avoid that.

But with growth, we discovered that we had to hire more outside helpers, at which time a problem evolved. It wasn't the cost; it was the nature of the care we were giving the children. While the quality of basic physical care was adequate, the motivation prompting it wasn't.

First, without recognizing it, we were treating the babies as a problem to be handed over to hired help. We weren't investing *ourselves* in our little ones—only our money. Second, we had to recognize that, even though the women we hired to do this job (nurses and, later, professional babysitters from a reliable agency) did it faithfully and well, they simply were not motivated or qualified to *minister* to the children in the power of the Holy Spirit. They watched them, but the Lord of the lambs wanted us to do far more than that.

John Farmer, a trained and efficient pastoral leader who organized and initiated our Christian education program (and serves today as our Executive Pastoral Administrator) came to my office one day.

"Jack," he said, "I believe we are to call upon the congregation to accept the care of the children in the nursery. When I was praying, the Holy Spirit brought to my mind Jesus' words about hirelings who do not care for the sheep as shepherds [John 10:11-14]. The ladies we have hired are dear women, but the sheep are simply not their proper responsibility. They are *ours* as a congregation. We have employed 'hirelings' to do our work."

He was right, no question about it. I considered the consequences. If we dropped the hired workers, we would have to ask the women in our congregation to rise to the task.

Quite honestly, I was bothered that they would miss some of the services. Not that I jealously wanted them to hear me personally, but I feared they would not grow, and that they might resent this intrusion on their freedom from childcare. God was asking me to implement something of the very ministry concepts I had been proclaiming. If I believed my own teaching, this was a chance to test its practicality.

As John and I talked, concepts about the nursery ministry took shape.

1. We were no longer simply to provide "childcare." Henceforth we would always speak of "child *ministry*." Whatever we provided as care must be accompanied by a sense and practice of ministering to each child. Even the babe in arms was to be prayed for, sung over, embraced as a lamb in the arms of another member of Christ's Body. From their earliest remembrances of being at church, we wanted our children to know the love and firm support of true fellowship in the Spirit of God.

2. Working in nursery or children's department service was "truly ministering." The words had to carry real meaning. Our understanding had to grow so that we saw the truth that lowly tasks are exalted in the Kingdom of God. Indeed, rocking a baby to sleep was quite as much a ministry as—and perhaps more than—standing in a pulpit to preach.

3. We had to establish a process of sensible training and sensitive rotation for the work. We mobilized and scheduled teams of workers so that no one would find himself interminably out-of-touch with the congregational worship and teaching, left in the nursery to wither spiritually.

Further, we sought to break any unwitting chauvinism among us that would have only women involved in this ministry. We have urged couples and men alone to join in the work of serving our children. While women still constitute the majority of our nursery workers, men—youth, singles, fathers and grandpas—are now a familiar part of the nursery child's life. At last count, nearly 100 men were helping in some aspect of caring for the tiny children.

In this way, young ones learn that Jesus isn't "just for women, children and preachers." And children with no man in their daily life have some contact with surrogate fathers who serve on behalf of "Abba"—Daddy God.

We decided to make the nursery ministry so effective and functional that no one would *not* want to use it for their children. In addition, we began to discourage parents strongly from bringing babies and small children into the services. The recency of birth, the unfamiliarity with the setting, the insistence of the parent—none of these argues validly against placing the child where it can be cared for in a manner and setting designed for its needs (although nursing mothers are seldom able to schedule feedings to allow their uninterrupted attendance for the 90 minutes of the service).

All of the congregation and most visitors cooperate agreeably with this provision; and if not, I as the pastor am rather forward on the subject. First, ushers and hostesses are careful to inform visitors with babies of the availability of the nursery. If they seem unwilling, they are asked to sit where they can move readily if the child creates a disturbance.

Most visitors understand and sense our love for the children. And even if on occasion I need to comment, we almost never have a problem in relating.

For example: A baby has fussed several times and the parents are doing nothing. "Mama or Daddy. That little tyke needs different care than either you or I can give him in this service. If I were he, I wouldn't want to listen to me, either."

Then I address the congregation as the parent begins to move from his seat with the child: "We love babies and children so much here at 'The Church On The Way' that we have gone to great lengths to guarantee proper service, care and facilities.

"Church, that child is a good reminder today that you are a key to ministering to our lambs. You can make no greater gift of yourself. If you've never done it, I encourage you to consider a place in the rotation schedule of the nursery. Or you can tend or assist in some other area in our children's ministry. The babies, the toddlers and the children deserve our best."

So it turns into a profitable encounter. But it *is* an encounter. It is not easy to invite someone to leave the service with a restless child, even though only a few are not sensitive enough to take the child out on their own accord when he is fussing. Those few can be addressed graciously.

It would be foolhardy of me to sacrifice an entire congregation's attention on the altar of one fussy baby or squirming toddler. Besides, it's not that folks want to be rude or stubborn. In most cases, even the charge of insensitivity is uncharitable. Parents—especially young parents—may simply not know what to do. They wilt with embarrassment as the child fusses, frozen in awkwardness and wishing the floor would swallow them up. In these situations, a few gentle words spoken by the leader can release the pressure, show understanding, and guide to a practical and comfortable solution.

A few idealists take exception, arguing that the value of the whole family's sitting together in church outweighs the disruption of sporadic cries from the infant or unwhispered comments from the restless toddler.

I disagree. It is silly to suppose the child views the situation in that light. From his view, he is being stuck into an adult situation completely unsuited to his interest or understanding.

And the other traditional way of handling problems—by providing small children with distractions—is unsatisfactory. Children who color or scribble their way through a childhood in the main sanctuary will become teenagers who goof off in the back row, and adults who, if they attend church at all, will have learned how to sit there and not listen. Every age group deserves a ministry geared to its capacity to respond and participate; and at "The Church On The Way," we insist that such ministry be available and used for the children.

This does not mean that children never participate in the life of the congregation as it gathers for worship. Each of their classes provide times for them to come into the services, prepared by their teacher as to what they may expect and how they can participate. Sensitive parents will also learn what pattern of progressive involvement works with each of their own children. Further, there are certain times each year when *all* of us assemble as a congregation.

But the general rule is departmentalization—not because we feel our little ones are an inconvenience, but because we know they are a priceless treasure, like precious stones that deserve a special setting to enhance their beauty.

## *Teaching Children*

Our basic curriculum of Bible training for the children is provided through our denomination's Christian educators in partnership with one of America's foremost evangelical publishers. It focuses on the Word of God, taught in a way that does not merely relay stories, but relates truth to life where the child is living it.

Simultaneous with each morning service, trained teachers administer a completely graded program of Bible instruction and practical teaching to our youngsters. Teachers are the key, since no curriculum can substitute for the spiritual preparedness, instructional thoroughness or personal interest of a committed teacher.

When we took our first step into multiple services in 1972, we were persuaded that the wisest step was to operate simultaneous Bible training programs during both services. This posed two questions: Would we need to double our teaching staff overnight? And what would we do with the children of parents who taught or attended our adult study before or after worship?

The latter question was solved easily. At first we thought we would need to prepare an alternative activity program for such children. We learned quickly, however, that the relatively few children in this category could go to the same class during the next service. This works because the classes are not actually "duplicates." The lesson is the same in content, but the teacher is new, as are most of the classmates. So these children expanded their relationships while they reinforced their understanding. (Later we developed our alternate program, but for years the above was effective—mentioned here to assist leaders wondering what to do.)

The former question was more difficult. Could we double the number of our teachers and still maintain the quality we enjoyed? The pastoral planning session in which we raised this question became silent. *Twice as many teachers*, we thought.

Then John Farmer looked up and said, "We need to pray. Jesus said He is the Lord of the harvest. If we ask Him to give us laborers, He has said He will do it."

Put simply, we did and He did. The Holy Spirit charged us with faith, and we had an old-fashioned prayer meeting there in my office. And God began to move people even before we announced the subject in public. I did alert the congregation to the need, but I employed no pressure or desperation tactics. The Lord of the lambs simply gave us people to help shepherd the young of the flock. He is still doing it where sensitive hearts keep available to the spirit of unselfish service.

People I meet in other parts of the nation sometimes ask me if we have a day school. We do not. That doesn't mean we're against the idea, just that, as of this date, God has not yet told us to. We have not set it as a goal, but believe we can reasonably expect to have one at the right time. Statistics show that when a child is schooled in an educationally sound and spiritually stable atmosphere, the results are superior in every way. This makes a day school a desirable product. Given adequate facilities and experienced leaders, in God's timing we shall pursue that ministry.

A day school should never serve parents who want to escape their own responsibility to "train up a child in the way he should go" (Proverbs 22:6, KJV). Nor should it isolate a child parochially from the world.

Since the day may well come when our congregation opens a Christian day school, we will make clear our unwillingness to substitute for a parent. No one should try to create an artificial environment in which to raise human flowers that cannot bear the heat of the hell raging around them in so much of the world. But the school can partner with parents in their task and help infuse children with character, insulating them against the negative forces of the unbelieving world. We must hold this delicate balance in dynamic tension. Otherwise a Christian school will become a monastery instead of a ministry.

## Kids of the Kingdom

I once heard Ruth Anderson, the Christian education director of the historic Moline Gospel Temple, say: "We must teach great truths to our little ones. If the world has learned to prepare meat in a form that can be spoonfed to infants, we must learn to prepare the meat of God's Word in a fashion the little child can receive. We cannot bring them as far as they need to go on milk only."

Our entire teaching program is characterized by that concept, but at no point does it come forth as emphatically as in our Wednesday night ministry. "Kids of the Kingdom" was conceived and birthed by Ruby Shoemake shortly after her husband, Chuck, began to help us on the staff. Other faithful workers from the congregation have advanced the original vision, and "KOK" has developed as a vigorous activity and training program.

We believe a child can learn to live and function in the full dimensions of New Testament life and truth, while becoming normal, sensible, happy kids. Consequently, we teach grade-school children to use the Word of God in faith, to receive the baptism with the Holy Spirit, to pray and to expect God to work daily and miraculously in their lives.

We do not believe that this will or should turn them into a set of religious oddballs. Balance, sensibility and the quality of

human wholeness in pursuit of supernatural possibilities—
the same life we teach adult believers—is the kind we teach
our children.

"Kids of the Kingdom" is loaded with action. Sports, games
and quizzes are all part of the two-hour-long evening agenda.
So is worship, prayer, meaty teaching, singing and further
spiritual guidelines on how a "kid" can live as a "Kingdom
person."

Jesus said, "Except you be converted, and become as little
children, you shall not enter the kingdom of heaven" (Matthew 18:3). At "The Church On The Way," we adults are
learning that pathway of humility; and among our greatest
joys is that of beholding our children as they begin to walk in a
similar spiritual maturity appropriate to their age.

The church must train its children, and it must give them
more than milk. Religious trivia, however apparently Bible-
oriented, will not satisfy the appetite or personal need of any
child. Our children—our lambs—are fed and groomed for
effective living in times that would otherwise overwhelm
them. They learn to "outlive" their counterparts in a rebellious
and morally eroded society.

Upon the birth of our first grandchild recently, Anna said to
me, "The baby's birth has reminded me of my own responsibility to our church's children." Shortly thereafter, "Grandma"
Hayford enlisted again for nursery duty. Through the early
years of four children of her own, and through all the years of
our earlier pastoral experience, she was a teacher and nursery
worker. It might well have been said, "She has served her
turn."

But "The Church On The Way" is the story of a people who
keep learning and who keep available to the Holy Spirit's
direction into ministry.

A quarter of a century ago, a young pastor's wife taught a
small class of children in the basement of a mission church in
Indiana. Since then she has done about everything in a church

that anyone could expect someone to do. Today she often does what no one would expect or require of her: she tends lambs in the nursery. And she's part of a congregation of people committed to caring for—ministering to—its lambs.

"Grandpa" and Pastor is proud of her, and of them.

# Chapter 13

# MEMBERS OF HIS BODY

She was sweet, beautifully simple and obviously sensitive. She had signed the visitor's guestbook in the foyer of the church, and I read her entry following the service, positioning myself at the door to greet the worshipers as they left. Beside her name, she had indicated as her church home, "The Body of Christ," and for the location of her church, "Worldwide."

I chuckled to myself as I glanced at her entry, but felt regret over the hollowness of the idea represented by this sincere young believer. It isn't uncommon to find people whose notion of membership in the Church is equally ethereal. And the saddest part is that such uncommitment is regarded by many as being of the highest order of spirituality.

I didn't say anything to her about it; I simply greeted her. And after we exchanged a few pleasantries about the service, which she admitted to enjoying, she was gone. I don't know that I ever saw her again. Perhaps she found a church home in time; but even so, I wonder if she would have joined.

The memory of that young woman has stuck for more than a decade, for to me she represents a contingent of believers truly devoted to Jesus Christ, but who never identify with His Body, at least in a local sense. That is, they never join a church.

Naturally, I'm fully aware of the wide spectrum of reasons for not joining a church. They range from scars yet borne by people wounded in former church relationships; to the casualties of denominational infighting, petty criticism and doctrinal accusations; to the domestic tragedy of divorce compounded by ecclesiastical ostracism. Other reasons for rejecting the idea of membership include miscellaneous opinions that generally reduce to something about membership as "a spiritual matter, not something written on a piece of paper."

I've pastored too long not to understand these problems. But I've also shepherded too long to believe that any sheep is safe without accepting the Holy Spirit's direction to settle down with one local flock and accept the care and feeding of one faithful pastor.

Meditating on the young woman mentioned above, and thinking how the Church is often referred to in military metaphors in Scripture, I have mused over the possibility of the following scenario:

*Location:* The streets of Manila, Philippine Islands.
*Scene:* A U.S. Military Police jeep stops, one of the patrol team jumps to the pavement and approaches an American soldier strolling unevenly down the sidewalk.
*M.P.:* [sharply] Soldier, halt! Where are you going?
*G.I.:* [muttering drunkenly] Nowhere . . . next bar.
*M.P.:* Looks to me like you'd better be headed back to your base. Where are you stationed?
*G.I.:* Nowhere in particular. Wherever.
*M.P.:* [to partner in jeep] This guy's spaced, Corporal. [to G.I.] Hold it, soldier. Again: Where's your base? Who's your commanding officer?
*G.I.:* Hey, man. I told you. [Stops, draws to full stature, mocks a salute.] I'm in the U.S. military, man. We're worldwide, haven't you heard? I'm stationed wherever I happen to go—in *the* Army, man. Global.
*M.P.:* You're drunk, fella. Where are your papers? Who's your commanding officer?

*G.I.:* The President, man. The Commander-in-Chief, like, you know, in D.C. at headquarters, man.

Enough. The whole proposition is bizarre, and if the situation actually occurred, there is no doubt where the soldier would be within fifteen minutes.

The irony of the analogy is its similarity to the thinking of many who, as innocent as they may be of the fact, are nonetheless ignorant of the biblical concepts of membership, submission to leadership, and union with a local assembly in abiding fellowship.

True, the Church of Jesus Christ is worldwide, and Jesus is the Lord—the Commander-in-Chief, if you please. But just as surely as a soldier in the U.S. military needs a base to ensure function and accountability, so an individual believer in Jesus needs identification with a local assembly. This is not a denial of our desire for unity with the global Body of Christ; nor is receiving the leadership of a pastor a substitution for the Lordship of Jesus in one's life. We're simply dealing with practical realities—and with the Word of God.

To become a member of a church is not a bureaucratic experience, it is a spiritual one; and at "The Church On The Way" we do our utmost to make it truly that. Since we believe that "joining" is a biblical term, we try to keep sensitive as to how we receive members that the Holy Spirit wants to add (or "join") to our body.

Just as a limb connects at a joint, so we believe the scriptural figure indicates that each member added to a local assembly is in fact *joined* with that assembly. We believe that temporal relationships are important for the season of Christ's purpose in our lives; that being knit to this local part of His worldwide Body is as specific and significant a placement as a physical transplant or as a military base assignment.

Ephesians 4:15-16 is graphic in its use of anatomical terminology:

But speaking the truth in love, [we] may grow up into him in all things, which is the head, even Christ: from whom the whole body fitly joined together and compacted by that which every joint supplieth . . . maketh increase of the body unto the edifying of itself in love.

These inspired words of Scripture teach a dependence upon one another that we ought to acknowledge—a dependence that results in healthy growth. Such is impossible unless a person commits himself to a local church.

Our need for fellowship is further underscored in I Corinthians 12:15-16. No one can properly say, "Because I am one distinct member [for example, an eye], I have no need of you." Nor can the issue be dodged by appealing to the context, found in verse 13—that since "by one Spirit are we all baptized into one body," therefore all other relationships are either unimportant or unnecessary.

In the same epistle, the apostle Paul teaches that submission to specific local leadership is important. The text discloses that even within the larger believing community of the whole city of Corinth, believers were aligned with specific smaller groups. Writing to believers in that city, he urged that every person submit himself to a spiritual leader who could be trusted. Paul used Stephanas as an example:

I beseech you, brethren, (ye know the house of Stephanas, that it is the firstfruits of Achaia, and that they have addicted themselves to the ministry of the saints,) that ye submit yourselves unto such, and to every one that helpeth with us, and laboreth.

(I Corinthians 16:15-16, KJV)

## Background on a Problem

The primary problem to some people who fear or resist commitment to membership in a local assembly is the fact that church membership is clearly not necessary to one's personal salvation. Some people who became members of a church before they were born again, never having been told the difference between a relationship with Jesus and a relationship to a church, are understandably wary. Now that they have found a meaningful relationship with Christ, they fear that formal membership might deprive them of something of the reality they now know in Him.

And because membership is often stressed in circles where vital spiritual experience is not, some of today's church leaders hesitate to even suggest the idea of membership for fear of seeming unspiritual. I had to work through that line of thought myself.

"After all," the argument goes, "since the true reality of membership is actually in the spiritual realm, why not leave it there? Forget the trivia of keeping books and rolls. Insistence on paperwork may just bewilder people. It might also discourage those who are finally tasting freshness and joy after years of barrenness elsewhere."

So fear posits itself, proposing that formal membership might taint a beautiful experience, hamstringing sincere people with human methodologies or organizational structures.

But this fear is rooted in the false supposition that publicly acknowledged church membership lies outside the realm of spiritual vitality; that it somehow binds spiritual relationship and fellowship with cords of nonspiritual institutionalized religion.

At first this sounds plausible, but it lacks either biblical or logical grounds. It is as unreasonable as refusing to plan a reception after a wedding because in some circles a senseless drunken brawl may mar it.

In fact, the reception of members into a local church family is not unlike a wedding reception. We are acknowledging each believer's union with Christ, and distinctly rejoicing that He has placed them in our local part of His great family. We welcome them to growth, fellowship and fruitful partnership.

What has already been accomplished when they vowed their lives to Christ we acknowledge; and we receive them openly and lovingly.

The Bible establishes this principle, and logic extends it. If "real" church membership (i.e., nonformalized) is too spiritual a matter to be sullied by institutionalization, what about "real" love and the civil rite of marriage? Is the texture of true love sacrificed when the vows are exchanged at the altar? Or when the documents are signed? Or when the union is recorded in the county courthouse?

Such views of domestic life are held today, of course, but not among believers who heed the Word of God. Thus, since a formal public commitment may crown a courtship and its season of romance, why cannot a public commitment to a specific church family enrich rather than diminish a person's experience with Jesus Christ?

Spiritual experience involves two things: an internal, private realization, and an external, public expression. When the Spirit of God draws us to faith and repentance, for example, we must express it openly through confession and baptism. The inner witness of the Holy Spirit, in other words, that we are indeed a child of God (Romans 8:16) does not conclude the case. Romans 10:9-10 calls for an enlargement of the circle of witness: "Confess with your mouth" as well as "believe in your heart." Following this comes water baptism, another public acknowledgment of an inner work of faith.

Since this pattern is so obvious with the birth of the believer, we may project the same pattern onto the believer's relationship with the church. When I am born into the family of God, I know so and say so. Similarly, when I find my place to live in that family, I should also know so and say so.

At "The Church On The Way," we are convinced that commitment to church membership contributes to the growth of a believer. While we by no means consider it essential to salvation, we have found that the act of commitment usually blossoms into new personal developments of ministry and

growth. When we receive members, therefore, we truly believe we are participating not in an institutional activity, but a
spiritual one.

Despite our deep convictions about the biblical basis and
practical wisdom of church membership, we never do anything to demand or promote church membership. Nevertheless, more than 4,500 adults and young people have submitted to membership in the First Foursquare Church of Van
Nuys since Anna and I joined as pastors in 1969.

My own understanding of the deep significance of this
practice grew with time, but not because I felt I had to answer
to a human or denominational tradition. In fact, I challenged
the idea with the Word of God. The way we began to receive
members was the result of my growing perception of certain
spiritual principles. Today we continue our quest to implement those principles with sensitivity, consistency and spiritual dynamic—a procedure born out of our early experiences
at the church.

By the autumn of 1972, the first full flush of growth had
come, and I was wrestling with the issue of membership.
Refusing to acquiesce to the idea that membership is unspiritual, I asked the Lord to help me perceive it from His
viewpoint. A biblical picture became my answer, helping me
to clarify the issue in my own heart.

In Israel and the Middle East, shepherds mark and count
their sheep—not necessarily to denote the shepherd, but the
owner. In the same way, we should be consistent to "mark"
and keep an accounting of our sheep, too. Jesus Christ was the
Lord, the Owner of the sheep, having bought them with His
own blood. But He had assigned certain sheep to my care; and
in order for me to know which are my charge, the mark of
membership becomes the point of accountability—for me and
for the sheep.

Thus, membership does not indicate ownership but corporate relationship. "I belong" could be twisted into a clique-ish

taunt, but our "I belong" has come to mean, "I am committed and I am responsible to."

With that view of church membership, we began to offer the possibility in this way:

## On Submitting to Membership

Many inquire, "How can I become a member of 'The Church On The Way'?" Answer: As an interdenominational fellowship in association with the International Church of the Foursquare Gospel, we stress open fellowship among the Body of Christ at large. We also stress the importance of identifying with a local assembly. So, if the Holy Spirit has made you a growing part of this assembly and you feel the desire to indicate your submission to Jesus' life in this circle of believers, Pastor Jack and members of the pastoral staff will meet with you on [date, place]. Membership requires that you:

1. Have received Jesus Christ as your Savior (John 3:3-5).
2. Agree with the church's statement of faith.
3. Will support the congregation's ministry with tithes, offerings and intercessory prayer.
4. Want to serve the Lord Jesus and will wait on Him to disclose to you your place of ministry in the ongoing life of our fellowship.

Until that time, we had asked those interested in joining the church to come to the office. Then we could arrange a meeting for new members and be fairly sure some candidates would be there. Now I was announcing a meeting without knowing who, if anyone, would come.

But they did come, and this approach has simplified the procedure and amplified the spiritual dynamic of receiving members.

I make no public announcements apart from the written notice, depending on the Holy Spirit to move people to acknowledge that He is drawing them to submit to and unite with this assembly. Then we can deal confidently and authoritatively with those who respond, for our base of authority is God's work in people's hearts, not our own solicitation or influence.

In even a passing mention of our "authority," I am inclined to wince, for the domination of some church traditions seems to me to have violated the Spirit of Christ and the intent of God's Word. Yet in the Epistle to the Hebrews, the practice of acknowledging one's submission to pastoral leadership is reinforced, at the same time emphasizing the awesome responsibility and accountability these leaders themselves will have before God:

> Obey them that lead you, and submit yourselves, for they are responsible to watch for your souls as ones who must give an account before God for their leadership responsibility.
>
> (Hebrews 13:17, paraphrase)

This Scripture notes that submittedness is required not only of the members, but also of the leaders. Pastors, elders or other officers are responsible to acknowledge their membership in a body, as well as their submission to its authority.

It is a worthy point of study to see how Paul, Titus and Barnabas submitted their flourishing ministry among the Gentiles to the evaluative, corrective judgment of the leaders in Jerusalem (Galatians 2:1-2, 9). Similarly, Paul and Barnabas gave an accounting to Antioch about the mission to which that church had commissioned them (Acts 14:26-28). They were not a pair of independent itinerants; they were accountable to their home base. They were not maverick evangelists beyond authority; they were sent from a home church.

When we teach about submission, we emphatically reject puppet-producing hierarchical authoritarianism. We do believe that each person's ministry is released most fully when that person is functioning under representative headship. This means that though the Lord Jesus Christ gives people to lead in His Church, they do not substitute for Him. Rather, they represent Him, and in that role provide an assisting head, a teaching voice and a leading example:

And He [Christ, the ascended Lord] gave some, apostles . . . prophets . . . evangelists . . . pastors and teachers . . . .
(Ephesians 4:11, KJV)

The elders which are among you I exhort . . . Feed the flock of God which is among you, taking the oversight thereof, not by constraint, but willingly; not for filthy lucre, but of a ready mind; neither as being lords over God's heritage, but being ensamples to the flock. And when the chief Shepherd shall appear, ye shall receive a crown of glory that fadeth not away.
(I Peter 5:1-4, KJV)

The headship, then, that Christ has placed *in* His Church as gifts *to* His Church is comprised of:

1. *Ministries,* qualified by gift and then placed by Jesus' own hand to assist His Body toward ministry (Ephesians 4:11-12);
2. *Elders* who feed and oversee the flock without selfish or material motivation, but by reason of spiritual commitment and maturity (I Peter 5:1-2);
3. *Shepherds* responsible to the Chief Shepherd who exemplify a quality of life to the sheep who follow them (I Peter 5:3-4).

## Reception into Membership

When people come to join "The Church On The Way," I emphasize that they are saying the Holy Spirit is leading them to do so, and that He has placed them here to work in coordination with the whole body.

Therefore, they are submitting first to God, second to pastoral leadership, and third to the local assembly. When they acknowledge their submission, I respond by submitting myself to them as well, for the Bible teaches that submission is the mutual responsibility of believers: "[Submit] yourselves one to another in the fear of God" (Ephesians 5:21, KJV).

I say to those who join: "I respond to your trust; and in submission to you as your servant and pastor, and on behalf of the pastoral staff, the elder body and the membership of the congregation, I make these commitments:

*Instruction:* "First, I commit myself to teach and feed you the pure Word of God (John 21:16). We who pastor you believe in the absolute need of your knowing and growing in the Word of God. We will give ourselves to nourish you, with the goal that you become the maximum possible person according to Father God's plan for your life."

*Correction:* "Second, in that same regard, we are committed to counsel or correct you, should you ever drift from the truth as it is in Jesus. The Bible directs pastoral leadership to 'reprove, rebuke and exhort with all long-suffering and doctrine' (II Timothy 4:2). We are committed to doing everything lovingly possible to keep you in obedience to the Lord Jesus Christ."

*Intercession:* "Third, we commit ourselves to pray for you. The Bible says we are to 'oversee the flock' and to 'watch for your souls' (I Peter 5:2; Hebrews 13:17). We will uphold you in regular intercessory prayer, the pastors and elders bringing your name before God's throne regularly."

*Protection:* "Fourth, we commit ourselves to stand by you in any time of need, burden or personal crisis. In the early church, 'no one said any of them that anything he had was his own' (Acts 4:32, paraphrase); and by that we understand that according to New Testament life, any material need you may have is ours to bear with you also. You are never alone if only you will let us know when need arises."

*Devotion:* "Fifth and finally, we commit ourselves to love you. Jesus said that this trait should mark His disciples (John 13:34), and we intend to live out that divine order of love. Its essence is not so much affection as commitment. Affection depends upon personal acquaintance; and, given time, we may enjoy growth in the purity and beauty of the acquaintance. But regardless of how close we become, we are always committed to you. Should you ever feel you have been hurt, neglected or misunderstood, you will know it is unintentional, for we will never do anything to violate you in any way. Our total commitment is to love, serve and help you become the person God created you to be."

*Reception:* With that, I conclude: "I extend the right hand of fellowship to you, and in Jesus' name receive you into this assembly. Please know that you are received." Then I embrace them, believing strongly that both the right hand of fellowship (Galatians 2:9) and the holy embrace (II Corinthians 13:12; *et. al.*) are spiritually dynamic expressions. If ministered in the power of the Holy Spirit, they establish a vital spiritual union between the persons being received and the assembly to which they are being joined.

## Responsible Membership

Most people do not join a church until they have attended for several months. This provides opportunity to understand the requirements and responsibilities of membership. Primarily, we expect people to give themselves to growth in Christ's purpose for them. We do not dictate how an individual should pursue this purpose. If He has called them to Himself and to this local fellowship, however, it follows that they will help in ministries that advance their personal calling and serve the congregation's need.

Here is how we relate our requirements and responsibilities for membership:

*First Requirement:* You must be born again, having received Jesus Christ, the Son of God, as your own Savior and Lord.

Corresponding responsibilities: To commit yourself continually to growth in Christ, and to be willing to pursue biblical standards of life.

*Second Requirement:* To be in agreement with the congregation's statement of faith, the Declaration of Faith of the Foursquare Church.

Corresponding responsibilities: To seek to live in the fullness of the Holy Spirit, the most excellent way to live in the truth you confess, and to manifest the fruit and gifts of God.

*Third Requirement:* To support the congregation's ministry continuously with your prayer, intercession, tithes and offerings.

Corresponding responsibilities: To accept a personal place in prayer and intercession, and to grow into the freedom of giving with at least the tithe as your starting place (Malachi 3:10).

*Fourth Requirement:* To wait on your ministry, seeking to discern the will of God for your life and service as part of this body.

Corresponding responsibilities: To be available daily as a Holy Spirit-directed minister of Christ's Kingdom; to abide in the fellowship of a church home group; and to help serve needs in the congregation.

If people have not yet been baptized in water, they are told that this will be expected as they become members. We do not require that one be baptized in *our* church, but we do teach and practice immersion after the person has received Christ.

We do not monitor the individual's response to these outlined guidelines in a demanding way. Our oversight is established for everyone's care, not to ensure their busyness. But
our requirements and responsibilities provide a clearly
marked pathway of expectation, and the majority choose to
pursue it, for they recognize it is founded on the Word and
ministered in a "living" way.

When we receive new members, two choruses underscore
the theme of our reception:

> We are bound to each other in love,
> By the words of the Father above.
> Through the blood of His Son,
> We are merged into one;
> We are bound to each other in love.
>
> —Eli Chavira

> It's a new and living way, walk ye in it.
> It's a new and living way God has planned.
> In this new and living way,
> I am walking day by day;
> Protected and led by His right hand.
>
> —Author unknown

It isn't difficult to maintain joy in a "joined" church relationship when that kind of love and that kind of life are the theme.

# Chapter 14

# "AS THE CHURCH AT ANTIOCH . . ."

God had said to me, "You don't believe you're in My will." I had been stunned. Then, in the ensuing years, He taught me what I have already relayed to you.

But in that 1971 midnight encounter with the Lord, which broke the back of poverty as a dominant attitude of control and self-protection, God addressed another subject that helps explain "The Church On The Way." It also expands on the practical nature of *relationships*, the healthy spirit of *inter-denominational love* and the wisdom of *firmly established commitment* to a local assembly.

These ideas are significant only if ministry is enhanced and enlarged by such attitudes, and we have learned they are. I was helped toward an openness to all that God wanted to do, by reason of something more He said besides what I related in Chapter Four.

That night, wrapped in my bathrobe and seated in the living room rocking chair at prayer, the Lord spoke to me. (At the time our congregation consisted of fewer than 150 members.)

*I will lift your voice as a congregation, and I will use this church to speak to your denomination and to the whole Body of Christ.*

By reason of God's earlier dealings, the moment had become too precious to laugh, but it might have seemed a mocking word. After all, I was an unknown pastor of a small assembly. But I had learned that when God speaks, there are three things to remember: First, do not challenge or resist the word; second, do not attempt to fulfill it yourself; and third, do not immediately or carelessly tell anyone else about it.

So instead of doing any of these things, I tried to sort out what had and had not been said.

First, God did not say that our church would be the only voice to our denomination. And, over the intervening years, confirmation has come. We have been privileged to influence our immediate Foursquare family circle. Our leadership has been honored and our words received. But there are many other congregations God has used in a great way to bless our denomination.

Second, God did not say that our voice to the whole Body of Christ would necessarily be recognized as such. Several months after this word from God, something happened to help me see more clearly the meaning of that aspect of His message to me.

The church council, our governing body, was at prayer one evening when I received a strong impression. I held back mentioning it for several minutes; but, recognizing the prompting of the Holy Spirit, I submitted the idea to the brothers praying with me.

"Men," I began, "I believe the Lord has given me a word, and I want you to judge it."

I was grateful to be speaking to men who support me lovingly, but who also would never rubber-stamp something I said just because they respect me.

They looked up, waiting for me to continue.

"I believe the Holy Spirit is saying this, regarding our church: 'I will make you as the Church at Antioch; and there will be ministries I shall lead out from this church that shall become better known than the church itself.' "

I was a little embarrassed. Not since my studies in college had I even thought about the biblical Church at Antioch. My memory was fuzzy, and I had little light to shed on what it might mean to be "as the Church at Antioch." In addition, I felt awkward about saying that ministries from the church would become *better known* than the church. It sounded as though we or I had been clutching for recognition. But both these matters would shortly be settled.

We took our Bibles and turned to the book of Acts, where I remembered the account of the revival at Antioch was recorded. Beginning in chapter 11, we read of the spread of the gospel following the death of Stephen and conversion of Saul of Tarsus:

> So then those who were scattered because of the persecution that arose in connection with Stephen made their way to Phoenicia and Cyprus and Antioch, speaking the word to no one except to Jews alone. But there were some of them, men of Cyprus and Cyrene, who came to Antioch and began speaking to the Greeks also, preaching the Lord Jesus. And the hand of the Lord was with them, and a large number who believed turned to the Lord.
>
> (Acts 11:19-21, NASV)

The ensuing verses and chapters record how Antioch became the first strong center of ministry in the Gentile world. In that place, ministries of many kinds evolved and were sent out:

> Now there were at Antioch, in the church that was there, prophets and teachers: Barnabas, and Simeon who was called Niger, and Lucius of Cyrene, and Manaen who had been brought up with Herod the tetrarch, and Saul. And while they were ministering to the Lord and fasting, the Holy Spirit said, "Set apart for Me Barnabas and Saul for the work to which I have called them." Then, when they had fasted and prayed and laid their hands on them, they sent them away.
>
> (Acts 13:1-3, NASV)

As we read these and other passages between Acts 11 and 16, we saw that something similar was happening in our midst. The Lord had already developed ministries that were beginning to be "thrust forth." Some, such as evangelists, musicians and teachers in the congregation, would go in and out, as Barnabas and Paul did from Antioch. Others, such as the young couples we were discipling for pastoral work, would go out permanently.

Then we gave thought to the seemingly peculiar words that many of these ministries would "become better known than the church itself." We meditated on the wisdom of that prompting, for it is not uncommon for a congregation with ministry that becomes known to be tempted to protect the prestige of that recognition; or, worse yet, to gloat over it. But as the Holy Spirit was broadening His definition of our call, He was helping us avoid any preoccupation with our own press notices.

As the years have passed, "The Church On The Way" has been reported more and more in the secular and religious news media, both local and national. But I revel far more in the many times God has allowed our church to minister in secret; and periodically I feel the need to exhort the congregation against any pride in being a member of "The Church On The Way."

In Revelation 3:1, Jesus scourges the Church at Sardis with the words, "Thou hast a name that thou livest, and art dead." Notoriety can endanger a congregation: "You have a name." May God deliver us from ever supposing that He is impressed with any recognition we may receive! Just as He delights to honor giving by the right hand that the left hand is unaware of, I believe He takes joy in honoring any congregation that will serve happily when no recognition is forthcoming.

In this regard, it is common for a congregation to be tempted to believe its strength lies in the fact that certain personalities of influence or renown are included in its ranks. That, of course, is a false premise; and Antioch is a case study of an admixture of influential people fulfilling their mission without the congregation's misplacing its identity.

A simple glance over the names listed in Acts 13:1 tells us enough to see that the Church at Antioch might have been inclined to think something of itself, if it had surrendered to the inclinations tempting some churches today. Barnabas was a big financial giver, and obviously a man of business experience and expertise (Acts 4:36-37). Manaen was from a world-famous family. Lucien and Simeon were well-recognized prophets or teachers in the Church of the day. And Saul—well, one can almost hear the words: "Saul of Tarsus is one of the members of *our* congregation! You know, the famous convert—former persecutor, conspirator, murderer of Christians!"

But the Antioch of Scripture seems devoid of such carnality. Instead, Acts 13:2-4 shows that congregation to have been given to *worship* ("as they ministered unto the Lord"), *intercession* ("and fasted"), *spiritual sensitivity* ("the Holy Spirit said . . .") and *ministry-mindedness* ("and they sent . . .").

The listing of specific men in this passage indicated to me part of what it must have meant to be "the Church that was at Antioch" in the first century. Also, it helped me to understand what it would mean when God called a congregation to be "as the Church at Antioch."

For God did indeed begin raising up men of renown, people of resources, capable ministries and individuals with dramatic conversions. And He was sending them forth in ministry—in many cases, taking people from unexpected realms of enterprise and making them "ministers" in unpredictable places accessible only through their particular vocation.

Like many churches, besides the effective influence and ministry conveyed every day by the ordinary worker, housewife and student, we have a large number of professional people who are touching the world at critically important places—attorneys, physicians, psychologists, professors, corporate executives, bankers, schoolteachers and the like. By reason of our location, on the border of the television, film and show industry, we also have a number of celebrities in our church. Within the congregation, this is no problem, since each individual is allowed to simply be part of the family. But beyond our congregation, this seems to become a fascination, if not a preoccupation.

Of course, we are not alone in this regard, for churches in various parts of the nation have well-known political leaders, famous athletes and entertainment celebrities in their congregations, too. Nevertheless, the degree of media coverage that our church has received, without explanation or quest on our part, has caused some people to think of it, mistakenly, as a "church of the stars"; and with equal misjudgment to suppose that renowned members are the reason for the church's growth.

I don't labor under either of these mistaken notions, which do not represent the ministry-mindedness of many of our better-known members, whose one goal is to take the life that Christ is growing in them as part of our body and serve others with it in their arena of influence. Nor do these notions represent an accurate commentary on God's grace in our congregation to suppose its growth is born of mere fame. Earthly glory in no wise compares with the heavenly order of blessing the Lord has showered upon us; and I am convinced that one of the reasons famous people are often drawn to "The Church On The Way" is because here a glory greater than the splendor the world offers is preciously present and fulfillingly abounding.

The Holy Spirit's attraction of famous people to our church is one of the ways the Lord has chosen to send forth ministries "that shall become better-known than the church itself." When some of the celebrities from our church sit on a star-studded talk show, and the "salt-of-the-earth" influence of their witness touches millions, no one knows or cares what church they go to. But Jesus has been shaping them for ministry in a twentieth-century Antioch, and it rejoices my heart to see any of our people fruitful in touching their sector of society with Jesus' life and love. (Incidentally, in our community so filled with musicians, actors, writers and other show business personalities, we are by no means the only church attended by several well-known people.)

The phrase *as the church at Antioch* essentially means two things: Commitment to ministry in worship and service, and commitment to being a center to equip and send people into the world. The systematic pursuit of doing exactly that keeps us focused on training *every* believer to become an agent of the Kingdom on a daily basis, as the Holy Spirit opens doors and enables their entry into each situation in Jesus' name.

Many beloved and well-known believers in our congregation have been part of fulfilling the Holy Spirit's word about sending out ministries from this church, but only a part. For that word has been fulfilled in many other ways, most of which remain unrecognized by either those who receive that ministry or by the majority of those who send it.

We do not make something grand of this ministry-sending task, but we do honor and accept the responsibility. We wait upon our ministry, as individuals and as a congregation; and when the Lord of the Church summons us into service, we are ready to respond. This congregation sends out ministry and supports those He sends by our hand, in whatever ways the Lord directs us to do.

Incidentally, at "The Church On The Way" we live by the same principle of submission I discussed in the preceding chapter. To function wisely and scripturally, individuals need to minister from the context of an established relationship with a local church. But I hasten to note that we avoid the rigid structures that some impose, either in high church ecclesiasticism or as taught by some charismatics in the name of "discipling." We believe that the submitted life is the secure life, freeing a person to live joyously and serve wisely.

This order of "submitted ministry" is biblically observable in the Church at Antioch. Although strong leaders flowed from this throbbing center of New Testament vitality, none functioned independent of the others. Paul and Barnabas eventually parted ways in Antioch (Acts 15:36-41), but the text does not suggest that either of them severed their rooted relationship with the congregation there. The submission of itinerant ministry to a local congregation is thereby illustrated in the Word of God.

The New Testament Church understood the wisdom and safety of mutual dependence for counsel and balance. Such submission does not deprive a person of his sense of God's direct leading. Instead, it provides a court of reference to which one can appeal for confirmation of what is valid, and for warning against what might be self-destructive. Such submission does not relieve anyone of his responsibility to mature in decision-making, but it can guard us all against the winds of confusion and error that might otherwise set us adrift.

The development and release of a person's ministry as a member of "The Church On The Way" is always nondominative. We apply principles of submission in the New Testament spirit of love and trust. We are careful never to extend our ministry or authority into any arena in which it is either inappropriate or uninvited. Those who request and accept our leadership will find it authoritative without being dictatorial. And those who would like us to serve them will find us available as proper order allows. We will care, but we refuse to usurp or intrude upon authority not vested in our charge to ministry.

Thousands have submitted themselves to membership in this congregation, and hundreds have gone forth in public ministry who yet continue in relationship with us. Scores of churches have either been born or strengthened unto growth by pastors sent from here. We have dispatched itinerant ministries in evangelistic, prophetic and apostolic works that have touched multitudes and edified churches.

Television and radio also help us serve the Body of Christ and reach people yet outside of Christ. The prophetic description of our church *as the Church at Antioch* has begun to be fulfilled, but we believe it is only that—a beginning.

"Antioch Revisited" is the theme of an article I wrote recently to the congregation, addressing them on our responsibility to prayerfully support those ministries Christ Jesus has sent forth from us. I could never have imagined the implications of what God spoke to me in 1972, nor can I yet envision all He still has in mind. But we do remain available to minister by His grace in those ways He opens, by directing and providing for them.

A fellow pastor expressed this recently when he said: "We want to minister to *everyone* we can, *everywhere* we can, in *every way* we can, *every minute* we can." The Church at Antioch worked toward this in the first century, and we believe the Lord wants every church to be "on the way" doing the same today.

# Chapter 15

# FOLLOWING THE RAINBOW

I had arrived late on purpose. The Sunday afternoon picnic fellowship had begun at three, and by the time I got there, well over a thousand of our congregation were already there with their children, and more were arriving.

It was the Fourth of July weekend, 1977, and following the morning services I had gone home to take a nap to refresh myself before joining the crowd at Emmaus Park—a ten-acre site we had purchased for gatherings such as this.

The festive spirit had to do with more than either the holiday weekend or the picnic setting; there was a joyous peacefulness that attends any situation in which God's people know they are giving themselves to His will in a conscious, concerted way. This gathering was happy and fun as well; but the sheer joy one could sense all over the park was clearly related to the fact that we were fulfilling a call the Holy Spirit was issuing to our congregation.

We were in the midst of the teaching series I had been bringing since my experience at the Shinjuku train station in Tokyo. The whole assembly was moving forward in the awareness that the Lord was calling us to reach outward, beyond ourselves. The progressive steps toward home groups were already in motion, and in one month we would launch that development.

But today—this very afternoon and into the evening—we were gathering in a park, having transferred our Sunday night service to this location. Our agreed purpose was to declare to ourselves and to the Lord our availability to move outward, away from a dependence upon our traditional site and into a dependence upon Him to make every place we worshiped a dwelling-place of His glory. We considered this event to be a statement: we were "on the way" in a new sense, with an expanding readiness to be what He was calling us to be, even when we were away from our home base.

There was a special exhilarating quality to the greetings I received as I walked across the grounds, meeting one nucleus of people after another. Smiles seemed brighter, embraces more loving. Indeed, though the words were not spoken aloud, a witness was being sensed by everyone present. The Holy Spirit was confirming the Father's blessing on our commitment to obey His present call to the Church.

I made my way to the pavilion area. About 300 children were being ministered to as Wayne Todd presented one of his priceless puppet shows, teaching dynamically, humorously and effectively, while captivating everyone present with the tender touch of grace resting upon his ministry. As I stood at the front door, carefully avoiding distracting anyone by being seen, one of the youth of our assembly ran up to me and laughed excitedly, "Pastor Jack, did you see the rainbow?"

My eyes followed her pointing finger to the multicolored arch directly overhead.

"It's just like the Lord is saying He's pleased, isn't it, Pastor Jack?"

I hesitated, not wanting to lend too much credence to a proposition that could be based upon mere happenstance; but then I smiled.

"Yes," I replied, looking up again intently. "It sure is."

And she ran on to others, leaving me there alone.

At that moment the Lord spoke to me: *Tell the people that it is true. The rainbow is a sign from Me. It is a response to their obedience, and a sign of My blessing upon them.* With that He impressed me strongly that I was now to tell them of His dealing with me the preceding Eastertide.

The night before Easter, just three months earlier, I had been kneeling at the rear of the sanctuary with the rest of the pastoral staff, as we sought God for His blessing on the services of the next day. As at other times, without premeditation and without warning, the Lord had spoken: *This will be the last Easter you will be in this building.*

*How peculiar,* I had thought, knowing there was no way we could have a new building built at this location in twelve months. But my concern was greater than the problem, and I prayed in response: "Lord, I don't know what You plan to do, but I do know this. Wherever You plan for us to be, my one request is that Your glory attend us there; for the only reason we have anything at all is because of that gift You have given us."

He answered me immediately: *My glory shall go before you. My glory shall rest upon you like a mantle. And My glory shall be your rereward.*

I wept.

And it was not until several weeks later that I told any of the pastoral staff of this prophecy, at which time we began to pray for God's guidance as to where our next Easter's meeting would be. But I had said nothing to the congregation. And now, as I looked upward at the rainbow, I knew I was to tell them two things: First, of that Easter eve word and its significance to our willingness to reach out through meetings beyond our church walls; and second, that the rainbow was God's seal of approval on our willingness to do so.

I trembled inside as I looked at my watch. It was 4:30, and in just one hour the crowd would gather on the grassy field for a time of worship and Communion together. I was under assignment to relate something I felt may well test the credulity of many of the people. For although we are people who believe in the supernatural, I have always been slow to assign too much significance to things that others might be gullible or superstitious enough to snatch as "signs."

My feelings were in conflict, much as Sheldon Vanauken describes his own when his wife was near death and a rainbow became an assuring sign of comfort to him. In his book *A Severe Mercy,* he not only relates feeling that assurance, but describes his intellectualized bouts over the feeling, and how he wrote his friend C. S. Lewis about it.

Lewis' answer characterizes the life and thought of that giant mind with the faith of a child.

> I can't now remember what I said in my lost [sic] letter about the "Signs." My general view is that, once we have accepted an omniscient & providential God, the distinction we used to draw between the significant and the fortuitous must either break down or be restated in some v. much subtler form. If an event coming about in the ordinary course of nature becomes to me the occasion of hope and faith and love or increased efforts after virtue, do we suppose that this result was unforeseen by, or is indifferent to, God? Obviously not. What we should have called its fortuitous effects must have been present to Him for all eternity.

Similarly, the Lord was assuring me that if I told the people what He was saying to me, He would bear witness that it was more than mere superstition.

The 5:30 worship began as one of our associate pastors led nearly 1,500 in singing and praise, and shortly I was on the platform beginning to lead toward the Lord's Table. The midsummer sun was lowering, but it would not set for more than an hour. The shadows extended long across the field, and I began by asking everyone to quiet their little ones and settle their children.

"One of our challenges as we move in ever-widening circles," I said, "into home groups and such times as these, will be the necessity for all parents to accept full responsibility to see that their children are orderly and not disruptive to the worship and teaching times. We'll always provide things that are relevant and meaningful to them, but this will also require their attentiveness."

The congregation stilled itself, and I set myself to deliver the message God had given me. I took time to express my natural reluctance to share what I was about to share. At the same time I affirmed my conviction that God wanted us to receive a confirming sign with the simplicity of children.

I related my experience of the past Easter season, and then began to describe the prompting He had given me earlier that afternoon—that the rainbow about 4:30 was God's sign to them, and that they were to receive it as such.

Then, with 1,500 people looking on, one of the most incredible events of my life took place.

It was just after 6 p.m., and I was retelling my conversation with the young person who had run up to me at 4:30. Everyone at the picnic had seen that rainbow, which had long since disappeared. Now, as I was reenacting the conversation, I came to the words, "I looked up to see the rainbow," and was about to say, "And the Lord spoke to me . . . ."

And at that moment, as I looked up, I saw *another* rainbow shimmering directly overhead! I was stunned. My speech faltered momentarily, every eye looked upward, and a holy murmur swept across the congregation. I fumbled for words, then invited everyone to kneel and worship the Lord.

While nothing foolish took place, it was not very neatly handled. I was overwhelmed. I tried to explain it all to the people but, while I was dissatisfied with my verbal attempts, there was no one present who did not understand what was happening. God was underscoring His promise to overspread us with His glory as we willed to obey His call for us to move outward with our witness.

That week I sought to express myself in a more reflective, coherent way by writing the following as something of a congregational journal entry, entitled, "I Believe in Rain-bows."

There are four instances in the Bible in which a rainbow is mentioned: three times in direct reference to the glory of God's presence and throne (Ezek. 1:28; Rev. 4:3; 10:l); and, of course, the best-known time—the manifestation to Noah after the deluge (Gen. 9:13-14, 16). The very fact of the references in each case indicates that the writers understood the rainbow to hold significance.

"Hey, wait just a minute. Don't you know a rainbow is just a natural phenomenon, nothing more than the spec-trum of color cast by the reflection of light rays passing through water vapor or crystals? C'mon now . . . you don't mean you believe they have significance! Only the simple would suggest any divine significance to rain-bows!"

But I do believe! Not that every one has a pot of gold at its end. Not that it's some kind of good luck sign. Not even that every time one appears there is some historic event to be recorded. But I do *believe*. I believe in rain-bows. Not only as scientifically explainable phe-onomena, but as spiritually accountable realities. Every rainbow has a message in it—at least one: that God in grace has promised to preserve mankind from a specific expression of His capacity to work judgment upon evil. And there is also an auxiliary message: God's promise is conveyed from one generation of the faithful to another, beginning with Noah, saying, "I am the Lord who has kept you thus far, and I will continue to do so."

As you know, Noah lived beyond the flood some 300 additional years. Can you imagine the remarks of succes-sive generations when heavy rains came: "It's happening again. Head for the hills!" But Noah knew better. He believed and spoke of the sign.

"Come off it, Mister," skeptics might have said a century or so later. Don't tell us that bow in the cloud means anything special. I suppose you expect us to believe God has spoken to you—you personally through that sign in the sky?" Turning one to another, they might have commented further, "Some people have the audacity to think that God would *bother* to touch the skies with a special message for them. The nerve . . . . Why, we've been seeing those things for—well, ever since I can remember—and we don't try and fill it with meaning! What a kook!"

Both Ezekiel and John viewed the rainbow around God's throne. They acknowledged it as a manifestation of His glory. And people could have told them, too, "You're seeing things." And that's right! They were. And they believed in the significance of them.

And so why should the rainbow over Emmaus Park last Sunday night mean anything to us? Why should I believe it was a sign of anything special indicating God's confirmation of blessing upon us at this stage of our corporate life? Should I just because there was a bow even without rain? Should I just because it appeared directly over the park—hardly appearing to be wider than the approximate dimensions of the site upon which we gathered? Should I just because it appeared just at the moment I was describing the unique gift of God's glory to us as a people? Should I just because we were gathered as we were as an explicit expression of our readiness to obey the Holy Spirit's directive that we extend our thinking and availability as a congregation beyond our walls?

I think so. And I do. I *do* believe God gave that rainbow to manifest His glory to the congregation, as a distinct sign of His readiness to work with power, because of our readiness to respond with obedience. And I believe that any time God gives a sign, it will take simplehearted faith to receive it with joy and confidence.

And I believe something else. I believe that the morning after the Red Sea parted, you could find several in the Israeli camp scratching their chins and with knowing, scientifically approved nods murmur, "It must have been the wind. How fortunate."

## Rainbow Fallout

What moved me most about the whole episode during the Fourth of July picnic was that it signaled a broader commitment on the Father's part to display His glory in an undeniable fashion. Just as He had shown that radiance to me one day in the sanctuary nearly seven years before, He now seemed to be indicating a new plateau of His intent to pour forth blessing.

The glory was not a private manifestation for the eyes of the leader alone, but for the people upon whom that glory would pour forth like heavenly radiation fallout, infecting each one with the righteousness and ability inherent in the presence of the King and the power of His Kingdom.

Moses said to the Lord, "I beseech thee, show me thy glory," and his face glowed with the impression of that encounter (Exodus 33:18; 34:29-35). Isaiah prophesied a greater day when the glory of the Lord would be upon every assembly place of God's people, as well as upon every home (Isaiah 4:5-6). When Philip said to Jesus, "Show us the Father and satisfy us," Jesus' answer was terse: "To look at me is to see the Father" (John 14:8-9, paraphrase).

Completing the cycle of revelation on this point, Paul states that as we, through the mirror of God's revealed truth, look upon the glory of the Lord in the Person of Jesus, it is thus, eyes upon Him, that we ourselves are being metamorphosed—i.e., progressively and relentlessly changed, transformed into Christ's likeness by the glorious liberating work of the Holy Spirit.

The flame over each head at Pentecost seems to be a distinctly personal manifestation of the same glory. Its presence testifies to the power of the Spirit to both *transform* and *transport*—to change each of us into the character of Christ and to charge us to touch others with the warmth of His love. "Rainbow fallout" is God's glory cloud distilling its vapor of beauty upon the head of each believer until our spreading witness fills the earth with His glory.

In sum, the glory is for every one of God's people, that all people may see the glory of God in their midst. The rainbow to us that evening was God's endorsement of a broadened commitment of one congregation to develop ever-widening circles by which His glory might be spread to others.

Isaiah 40:5 is more than a promise; it is God's revealed purpose: "And the glory of the Lord shall be revealed, and all flesh shall see it together" (KJV). He wants all His people to taste His glory, that they might show it to the nations, beginning next door.

## More Rainbows

That wasn't the end of it. Nor was it the beginning of a surge of frantic searchings for signs—rainbows or otherwise. But on at least two other occasions, rainbows appeared at precise times and without natural explanations (since neither occasion was a rainy day).

The next time was at the beginning of our first Easter service away from the congregation's home base in Van Nuys. We had secured the use of the stadium at California State University in Northridge. It was a venture in faith to wean a congregation from their traditional place of meeting, especially on the day of resurrection celebration.

But it happened! And while the stands were filling with more than 5,000 and overflowing onto the field, a rainbow halo circled the sun. I didn't say much about the sign in the sky, for many visitors wouldn't understand its history or present significance to us. But the congregation smiled and rejoiced knowingly. When the message concluded, more than a hundred received Christ as Savior. And God had put a rainbow seal on the whole package!

Then there was the Day of Ingathering. Midway during the building of our new Living Room (multipurpose sanctuary/concert hall/dining room/classroom), we obtained legal permission to meet one Sunday in the unfinished building. We gathered under open skies, surrounded by the newly erected walls that established the perimeter of the structure in progress toward completion.

Six weeks earlier I had written the people, sharing with them a summons to faith that had stirred my own heart. "Let us come to one great Sunday of giving," I had written, "bringing a special offering of Ingathering to hasten our new building on to its finish."

Being wary of goal-setting, I didn't tell them what I inwardly believed God had promised me: that if I would summon their giving in this manner, He would stir their hearts, and one million dollars would be committed in one day.

Tables were set up everywhere as the congregation gathered that morning. Everyone sat like schoolchildren at desks facing the temporary platform mounted for the occasion. Our regular four-service schedule was in effect, even though the much larger area was in use. With the tables spread as they were, there was a comfortable feeling that we were beginning to actually occupy our new family dwelling.

One of our members had come to me a few days before. "Jack," he said, "I was reading the other day of the Lord's instructions to Israel to write His Word upon their doorposts. I felt prompted to ask if you felt it might be a good thing for the people to write promises from God's Word on the open studs in the new building, as a part of the service for Ingathering Sunday."

My heart leaped. Absolutely!

Such practices may strike some people as sensational, emotional, sentimental or stupid. But bypassing these accusations, and confident that our convictions are based in the reality of the invisible, we not only covered the studding with the Word of God, but were honored by God with another rainbow.

And not just one. The fact is, in three of the four services that morning a rainbow appeared, once on the horizon and twice overhead. I chose not to make a great issue of it, but I also chose to acknowledge my belief that God was further confirming His pleasure with our direction and His promise to accompany us forward. (And incidentally, the total offering and commitments came to exactly one million and *six* dollars!)

## Risking Belief

One is always at a risk to believe in the invisible. Even when the visible evidence confirms your belief in "invisible means of support," it is judged by many as not intellectual enough, somehow. And it is unscientific or fanatical when someone says he believes and travels in what others may not judge to be approvable terrain.

A scientist is charged as being inconsistent with his profession when he expresses belief in a personal Creator. A doctor may be thought mystically errant if he refuses the spiritual cynicism that can so readily tempt those esteemed medical servants who toil against the seemingly relentless, apparently random and horribly unjust toll taken by disease, affliction, pain and death.

Even a pastor becomes vulnerable to accusations of unorthodoxy if he ventures too far into the arena of belief in the invisible. Many of his peers will allow a measure of faith in the unseen; but even in the circles of those whose stock-in-trade is supposed to be "the spiritual," there is an uneasiness if too much is claimed.

This doubt is explainable. Soothsayers, charlatans and kooks are present in large enough numbers, making wild enough claims, that it seems logical for someone who has had a *bona fide* spiritual experience to remain reluctant to relate it.

But all this notwithstanding, the evidence mounts, and one comes to the place that he, as I, must risk being bold enough to tell it outright. In the telling, one determining distinctive distinguishes our record from mere sensationalistic gullibility.

Throughout this book, I have anchored every experience in the Word of God—the timeless, eternal Scriptures. The pages of the Bible are laden with episode upon episode of signs, wonders, prophecies, healings, God speaking with men and women, angels at work, miracles, glory clouds, and . . . rainbows.

In concluding with the "rainbow experiences," I have done as before, showing the consistency with the Word of God and with the testimony of proven, faithful believers. But I haven't discussed an abiding principle, for in the most obvious respect there is no "New Testament Principle of Rainbows"—i.e., no pattern to "live in" or pursue ongoingly.

Or is there?

One of the scientists in our congregation wrote me one day following one of the rainbow occasions. Here is what he said:

> Pastor, the whole idea of a rainbow is based around the light of the sun being projected toward a man in a straight line—the axis of projection. If we consider the possibility that the sun may serve as a type or symbol of God, projecting in a straight line—His Truth—to mankind as a promise, then here are some randomly ordered analogies that might illustrate the spiritual significance of a rainbow:
>
> The intensity of a rainbow is directly related to the number of raindrops present—the more, the brighter; it is only when a large body of raindrops are seen together that a rainbow can be detected. It is a collective phenome-

non, obviously a message on the need for the spirit of unity in the whole Body of Christ.

All colors are present in the "white" light of the sun, but white light is refracted—bent—as each believer receives the full glory of God. There is a lesson of God's grace in the fact that each raindrop "bends" the light. All of us, in a sense, due to our sinful nature, bend God's light that impinges on us. Yet, God is still able to turn that refraction into a work of beauty (Romans 8:28).

He is doing this through the Body of Christ, the Church, constituted of millions of people who are like raindrops through whom the Father is showing forth His glory. To emphasize this need for unity in the Body of Christ, we might learn from the fact that each individual raindrop projects the full spectrum of light, but will only appear as reflecting one color depending upon the observer's point of view. How different each of us appears to one another! And yet, when the whole rainbow is seen by reason of a multitude of drops, the diversity of colors shown is always orderly—in the same consistent relationship to one another—and is beautiful to behold.

He included a number of other observations, including the scientifically established technicalities of the position of the sun with reference to the horizon, and the angle between the sun and the observer. The practical significance of these facts is in the issue of the timing involved in the appearances we saw. There were simply too many occasions, too many variables and too little capacity of man to manipulate such appearances—all of which argued convincingly that it took more faith to doubt the "rainbow message" to us than to believe it.

In the final analysis, however, we aren't basing any of our past or our future on anything so ephemeral as a rainbow. The roots of our faith are in the Word of God; the Light of our world is the Son of God. That we may be likened unto transient raindrops is perfectly acceptable, for ours is only to be, like waters from a fountain, caught up by Himself and poured out where He wills.

The glory keeps shining, and the reason we are a congregation "following the rainbow" is that He has made us part of that worldwide collective Church He is using to manifest Himself to the world today. The glory is His, for He is the source of the light. But the privilege is ours to receive and disperse that light.

And as we do, we keep "on the way"—sometimes being caught up to Him in worship, even as waters are evaporated to the heights; and sometimes being poured out in service, even as rains are sent from the skies.

The glory of God shining through frail, transient humanity is reminiscent of Paul's description of the ministering Church—the words I used as my text that first night at the church so long ago:

But we have this treasure in earthen vessels, that the excellency of the power may be of God, and not of us.

(II Corinthians 4:7, KJV)

Wherever God can find people who will understand and respond to that call and on those terms, you will have a church "on the way"—in His way.

And there will be rainbows.